PEOPLE OF WIGHT

To Hugh and Anne.

I hope you enjoy the book and thanks very much for your support.

Angela

PEOPLE OF WIGHT

ANGELA WIGGLESWORTH

Foreword by Cliff Michelmore

ALAN SUTTON PUBLISHING LIMITED

First published in the United Kingdom in 1996
Alan Sutton Publishing Limited
Phoenix Mill · Far Thrupp · Stroud · Gloucestershire

British Library Cataloguing in Publication Data

A catalogue record for this book is available from the British Library

ISBN 0-7509-1091-7

Cover illustrations: front: The Needles and lighthouse. The name is said to come from the 120 ft high needle-shaped rock known as Lot's Wife, which collapsed into the sea in 1764. Its base can still be seen at low water. The lighthouse, built in 1859 and 109 ft high, is at the end of the most westerley rock (*photo*: The National Trust). *Inset, top:* Rachel Thomas (*photo*: Ian Pert); *bottom:* Paul McKillop (*photo*: Angela Wigglesworth). *Back:* A field of poppies (*photo*: The National Trust).

Unless stated otherwise in the Acknowledgements, all photographs remain the property of the author.

Typeset in 10/12pt Times.
Typesetting and origination by
Alan Sutton Publishing Limited.
Printed in Great Britain by
Ebenezer Baylis, Worcester.

Contents

Acknowledgements

I would like to thank Gay Baldwin for her invaluable checking of the manuscript, Jane Jones of Isle of Wight Tourism for helping with my initial research, and Wightlink Ferries for their assistance with transport to the Island.

I would also like to thank all those who kindly gave me their time; without them I would not have been able to write this book.

My thanks, too, to the owners of the photographs on pp. 1, 2, 25, 27, 32, 62, 63 and 137 for allowing me to use them. I am also grateful to the *Isle of Wight County Press* (pp. 65 and 100), English Heritage (p. 2 of colour section), and The National Trust (main front and back cover pictures and p. 3 of colour section) for permission to reproduce their photographs.

Angela Wigglesworth
1996

Foreword

'Wherever we come and which way so-ever we look we see something new, something significant and something well worth the traveller's stay and the writer's care,' wrote Daniel Defoe. Now if that traveller had crossed the waters and stayed a while he would certainly have found many things worth his while and significant. In the first place he would have heard the natives referring to the Isle of Wight as the definite article. The Island, as though others hardly mattered, and of course to those of us who were fortunate enough to be born and brought up here they don't. Other islands are merely compared with ours: 'Malta, is half the size of . . .'; 'Barbados is little larger than . . .'. But size is of little concern to most visitors, many of whom arrive knowing only its famous landmarks and attractions: Carisbrooke Castle, Osborne House, The Needles and coloured sands of Alum Bay, Tennyson Downs, the resorts of Ryde, Sandown and Shanklin, the gardens at Ventnor and the

A relaxing moment at Bembridge Yacht Club.

yachts at Cowes. Others come for the birds at Newtown Creek, the dinosaurs at the back of the Wight or to hop around the harbours of Bembridge, Yarmouth and Wootton Creek or to walk the coastal paths. Seldom do they really get to know many of the people whose lives are rooted on the Island.

When I recollect my own childhood at Cowes in the '20s and '30s, it is the people I most readily remember. Freddy Stainer, his basket at his hip, having great difficulty crying 'Fresh watercress' because of his cleft palate; Mr Finch smilingly dispensing his cream ices; the schoolmastering of Guppy and Waller, Capps and Mackenzie and the footballing of George Reader and Joe Butchers at Westwood Park. In high summer there was always Wagstaffe, the signalman at the Royal Yacht Squadron, firing the guns to start the races in Cowes Week and in the winter Mr Shergold provided us with the warming smell of roasting coffee beans that drifted up through the grill in the pavement in front of his shop up Shooters Hill. All people I can visualize to this day.

There are those who insist on crying for an age that is past but I am not in their number. In the compilation of this book Angela Wigglesworth could so easily have picked up dozens of old characters who would have looked back on times past and times remembered, but she resisted the temptation if indeed she were so tempted. What we now have in *People of Wight* is a collection of interviews with a broad sweep of people, young and old, Caulkheads and Overners but all with a story to tell. Many of them I have known most of my life, others I have only met here for the first time but I am well aware that Angela has listened sympathetically and wisely to each and every one of them. What we are left with is a valuable social document and a commentary on the people who live and work on the Island in our times. I trust that you will find them as entertaining and enlightening as I have done.

Cliff Michelmore
Bembridge
1996

Brief History

1900 BC. The Beaker people, a Bronze Age race, arrived. Their name derives from the distinctive pottery drinking beakers they left behind. They called the Island 'Wiht' (weight), meaning 'raised' or 'what rises over the sea'.

AD 43. The Romans arrived and translated 'Wiht' into Vectis, from the Latin *veho* meaning lifting. They ruled peacefully for 400 years.

530. The Saxons arrived. A period of strife followed.

686. Caedwalla, the West-Saxon king, conquered the Island and introduced Christianity.

897. The Danes arrived, 'burning and killing' for over a hundred years.

1066. The Normans came and a peaceful 300 years followed. William the Conqueror gave the Lordship of the Island to William FitzOsbern, who transformed the fortress at Carisbrooke into a Norman castle.

1293. Isabella de Fortibus, Lady of Wight, on her deathbed, sold the independent Island for 6,000 marks, to Edward the Confessor. Edward retained the Lordship, and appointed 'custodes' to administer the Island for him.

1377. The French destroyed Yarmouth, Newport and Francheville (renamed Newtown in Tudor times).

1444. Henry Beauchamp, Duke of Warwick, was given the title of King of the Isle of Wight by Henry VI, who attended the ceremony.

1509. The title of 'Lord' was changed to Captain, and later became Governor and Captain. During Henry VIII's Dissolution, the king had Beaulieu Abbey destroyed and used the Caen stone to build castles and forts at Sandown, Ryde and St Helens.

1545. Sir Richard Worsley, Captain of the Island, fought off the last French attack. Yarmouth Castle was built.

1599. The population of the Island was under 9,000; six representatives were returned to parliament.

1647. Charles I became prisoner in Carisbrooke Castle, from where he was taken to be executed in London in 1649.

1771. A House of Industry was built at Parkhurst to provide work for the Island's poor, the first workhouse in Britain. It closed in 1836.

1785. The first lighthouse was built at The Needles; a new one was erected in 1859.

1814. A wooden pier was built in Ryde, the first in Britain.

1820. The earliest recorded steam ferry service to the Island began, from Southampton to Cowes, with a three hour crossing.

1845. Queen Victoria and Prince Albert bought Osborne Estate. Osborne House became the family home from 1846 until the queen's death there in 1901.

1853. Alfred, Lord Tennyson rented Farringford, and later bought the house with the profits from his poem, 'Maud'.

1859. The present Needles lighthouse, 109 ft high, started working on 1 January.

1862. The Lower Needles Battery was built as part of Lord Palmerston's coastal defences. The first railway on the Island was opened between Newport and Cowes.

1869. The Royal National Hospital for Consumption and Diseases of the Chest was built in the Undercliff on the site of the present Botanic Gardens.

1880. The tramway from Ryde St John's to the Esplanade was replaced by a railway which continued to the end of the pier.

1886. Ryde tramway was electrified, one of the first electric railways in the country.

1896. Princess Beatrice, Queen Victoria's youngest daughter, became Governor of the Island, and lived in Carisbrooke Castle until her death in 1944.

1897. Guglielmo Marconi transmitted his first wireless broadcast from Alum Bay and set up the first permanent wireless station in the world.

1898. The first medical bulletin ever transmitted by wireless was sent from the Royal Yacht to Osborne House.

1908. Barnes Wallis, designer of the Wellington Bomber and the Bouncing Bomb, came to work for J. Samuel White at Cowes.

1939–45. Over 10,000 buildings were destroyed or damaged on the Isle of Wight during the Second World War. Saunders Roe produced 800 aircraft here.

1955–71. The Needles Headland became a top secret space missile testing site for the British atomic missile and space rocket programme. In 1971 the first and last all-British satellite (*Prospero*) was launched from here by a British rocket. *Prospero* should remain in space until the year 2200.

1959. The first prototype hovercraft was built.

1962. The SRN2 Hovercraft carried fare-passengers between Ryde and Southsea, and became the first commercially operated hovercraft in the world.

1965. Admiral of the Fleet, the Earl Mountbatten of Burma, a great-nephew of Princess Beatrice, was appointed Governor and later Lieutenant of the Island.

The first Islander plane, built on the Island, completed its seventy minute maiden flight on June 13.

1972. The Island gained full county status under the Local Government Act.

1973. The chairlift opened at The Needles Pleasure Park.

1979. Earl Mountbatten was killed.

1995. The Isle of Wight became a unitary authority.

Introduction

The Isle of Wight lies off the south coast of Hampshire and is the smallest county in Britain. Diamond-shaped, it stretches 23 miles from west to east, 13.2 miles north to south, has a population of 123,000 and all its towns are on the coast except Newport, the capital, which is in the centre. It has three rivers and 500 miles of roads of which half a mile is dual carriageway. It has its own Governor, appointed by the Queen, and there are no party politics in town or parish councils. In April 1995 a single unitary authority (replacing district and county councils) was set up but it is not, as some think, the first in the country. The Isles of Scilly have had such an authority since 1881.

Each year 2.3 million people visit the Isle of Wight, of whom 1 million come for the day. The quickest journey (ten minutes) is by Hovercraft, the longest (fifty-five minutes), the boat from Southampton to East Cowes. Wightlink and Red Funnel both operate ferries at frequent intervals during the day and some during the night. There are said to be more 'attractions' on the Isle of Wight (castles, museums, medieval manor houses, craft centres, vineyards, country parks, Roman villas) than in any other area of equivalent size in Britain or, as one enthusiast suggested, the world.

Even before Queen Victoria and Prince Albert came to live in Osborne House in the 1840s and the great flocked to see them, poets, artists and writers had found the Island a place to visit for health and inspiration. 'The air is commended both for health and delight,' wrote a seventeenth-century author. 'The first is witnessed by the long continuance of the inhabitants in the state of their bodies before they be decayed. And the other for quality gives place to no neighbouring county.'

Wordsworth came in 1793 and stayed in Carisbrooke Castle; J.M.W. Turner painted his first oil study here, a picture of fishing boats off The Needles; Keats stayed in Shanklin and wrote 'St Agnes Eve' (although he confessed in a letter to a friend, he was getting 'a great dislike of the picturesque'). Tennyson lived in Freshwater for many years; Dickens wrote part of *David Copperfield* in Bonchurch; Macauley spent the summer of 1850 working on his *History of England* and Karl Marx made three trips to Ryde and Ventnor and described the Island as 'a little paradise'. Liszt played the piano in a Ryde pub; Disraeli came to pay his respects to Marconi, and George Eliot wrote in a letter to a friend that 'the place is perfect . . . in its combination of luxuriant greenth with the delights of a sandy beach'. George Bernard Shaw and T.S. Eliot both spent their honeymoons in Freshwater and J.B. Priestley lived on the Island for many years. It seems they were all bewitched by what the place had to offer, and today writers, politicians, broadcasters and actors alike continue to make it their home.

One can almost sympathize with Hester Thackeray Fuller who wrote in her book, *Three Freshwater Friends* published in 1933: 'Is there no one who is commonplace here? Is everybody either a poet or a genius, or a painter, or peculiar in some way?'

When I started writing this book, people from the mainland smiled nostalgically at the memories of happy childhood holidays they'd spent on the Island. But there's more to this island than good beaches. It is a very beautiful place with forests, woodlands full of bluebells and primroses in flower several weeks before those on the mainland, open downland with wonderful views of the sea. There are pretty thatched-cottage villages and timeless tea gardens. Over 200 species of birds have been recorded here, it is a stronghold for the red squirrel, and it is the only home in this country to the Glanville Fritillary butterfly.

There is relatively little crime, and people are more relaxed than on the mainland ('later' can mean a couple of weeks). There's a friendliness in the shops typical of an island community, although Overners (people born on the mainland) and Islanders (born on the Island) know they'll never be Caulkheads (those born on the Island with several Island-born generations behind them). The local accent is difficult to define. A mixture of Devon and London, someone said. There's not much left of Island dialect though some words still survive, like nipper (anyone aged 8 to 80), nammit (a snack), mallishag (caterpillar), galliwagger (scarecrow). If you manage to say 'dain Cayees' (down Cowes way) the right way, you might almost be considered local.

The Island has its problems of course. It has the worst unemployment figures (11.2 per cent) in the south of England; many resent the lack of government funding that could encourage more businesses to be set up here, and regret the lack of investment in existing industries. 'There's no work other than seasonal for most young people,' said Simon Goodenough, curator at the Botanic Gardens, 'but many don't want to leave the Island. They feel there's security here. Some, of course, are lured by the faster pace of the mainland, they can't wait to get there, but then find they can't cope because it's something they're not used to. By and large, children whose families have lived here for many generations, don't want to go.'

New multi-national stores in Newport are welcomed by some, but as everywhere else, they've forced out the smaller shopkeepers. The ferry to the mainland is considered too expensive, and an issue that has been argued over since the turn of the century and probably before, is that of building a fixed-link to the mainland. In a book published as early as 1904, the author wrote: 'A proposal has been made to connect the Isle of Wight with the mainland by means of a railway tunnel under the Solent . . . this tunnel and electric tramways are likely to be constructed before long.' Needless to say it has never been built and in a recent survey carried out by the *Isle of Wight County Press*, two to one residents are against the idea.

The Isle of Wight today is a surprising place. It's well loved by the holiday-makers, of course, but how many know, for instance, that the only commercial garlic-growing company in the UK is based here, and the only company in Europe making paragliders? That a large branch of Westland Aerospace operates from East Cowes? That the Islander

A Red Funnel ferry sailing past Cowes.

plane (used worldwide) was invented and is still being assembled at an airfield near Sandown? And that Siemens Plessey make their multi-million pound radar systems here?

Many books are published every year about the Island's past. This book is about the present, about the people (Caulkheads, Islanders, Overners) of all ages who make the Island what it is today. Over ninety of them (and I would like to have included many more if this could have been a bigger book) talk about their work, their concerns for the future, and the good and bad things about living on an island that is only ten minutes away from England's south coast, but which has managed to retain a gentler pace of life than now exists in most of mainland Britain today.

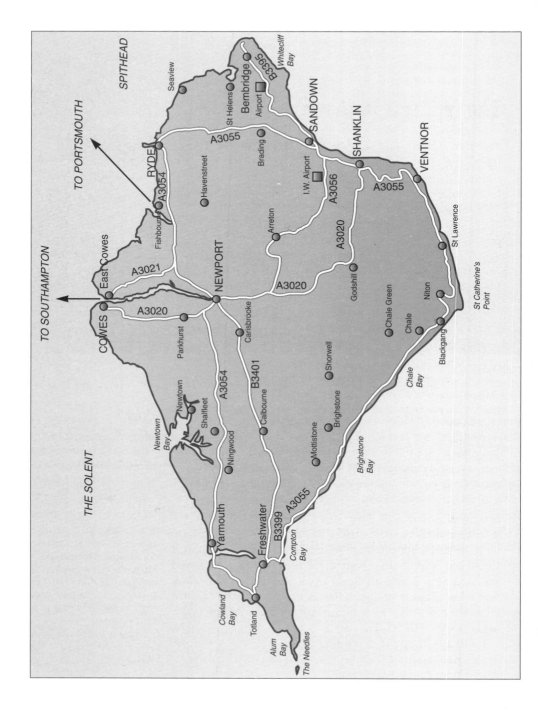

The Village Policeman

There are about nineteen village policemen on the Island. Each major town has its own station, but to give community contact, each village or group of villages has a local policeman and when he's not about, calls go to policemen on patrol.

I have a little Honda 250 motorcycle, but if I want to walk or ride my bicycle, I do. They don't mind what I use as long as I can be contacted on the radio. Normally I ride my most modern bike, that's a 1955 one. If you're in a car, you're in a little box and feel cut off and I find it's always enjoyable to talk to people about their hobbies and interests.

It's surprising how busy we can be at times – the Island's a holiday location, of course, and we get a lot of people coming for summer work. Youngsters who perhaps have been in trouble in other parts of the country come for a season's work and then think, well, they might as well be on the dole down here as somewhere up north. In fact, the Isle of Wight is the fourth busiest division in the whole of Hampshire and that includes places like Southampton, Portsmouth, Basingstoke and Aldershot. The Island's not as small as a Scottish island where everyone knows everyone else, and where you have anonymity, people will commit offences because they think they're not likely to get caught.

But we don't get the same level of violent crime that occurs in cities, and it's a bit of a shock when you have your first robbery. I remember my first one here. The guy with the funds set off for a holiday in Majorca. The police found out who it was, waited for him to come back and arrested him. Then all the money was recovered stuck under his mattress at home. But things have changed since then. We had those big fire bombings which you just don't expect on the Isle of Wight.

I always thought I wouldn't want to be a village policeman, that I'd like to live some way from where I worked, but there hasn't been any problem being here in

Tony Dymott, 40, was born in Southampton, and worked in a chemical laboratory before joining the police force in Bristol when he was 20. He came to the Isle of Wight about ten years ago and now 'looks after' Binstead and Havenstreet. He has a collection of thirty antique bicycles, tricycles and tandems, including an 1833 Penny Farthing and a Macmillan machine he made himself, a replica of the first-ever wooden bicycle. He is married to Janine who was born on the Island.

the village, though I get occasional phone calls and some visitors at the door. We've had a run of found dogs recently, so I've put a cage by my gate and if anyone has lost one, they can come and see if it's here. For getting to know people, you can't beat working and living in the same area though I did once have to breathalyse my next-door neighbour. But if there is something sensitive, I can always pass it on to a colleague. You're bound to build up social friendships and sometimes, someone you know finds themselves on the wrong side of the law. All you can do is try and be as fair and reasonable as possible, and knowing them can be an advantage. When you walk through the door, you're not a stranger and that takes down a lot of barriers.

I like the fact that people know me, know my first name and, hopefully, I can remember theirs. There *is* a sense of community here, and I think that's nice. With 3,000 to 4,000 people, I can get round on foot or bicycle reasonably well. But if I'm desperate – there's an intruder on the premises, or a nasty domestic situation rapidly getting out of hand – I can dump the bicycle and flag down a passing car, which I've done on quite a few occasions. I've never been refused so far. I think the drivers are so relieved they haven't done anything wrong, they're only too happy to give me a lift.

The Bus Driver

I drive all types of buses, but mainly double-deckers and in the summer we have the Island Explorer with a PA system so we can talk to the public as we go along. I like that because people should know where they are. I always give them a bit of information and they do appreciate it.

I know my regular passengers more by their faces than their names and I've always got on very well with them. This morning I started collecting for the Rotary Club's Ryde Festival, and would you believe it, I've collected £100 already in sponsorship. I put a tin on the bus and they put money in. 'I can't pass you by,' they say.

I like to have a laugh and talk with passengers and when they get off I say, 'Cheerio, dear, I will see you later, don't forget to get the steak and chips ready'. And somebody says, 'Is that your wife?' and I say, 'No, I'm only joking'.

Walter Charles (Wally) Edwards, 62, came to the UK from Jamaica in 1958. He worked as a bus driver in Southampton, the Isle of Wight and Oxford before returning to the Island in 1961 to work for the Southern Vectis Bus Company. He is a magistrate and a member of the Board of Visitors at Camp Hill Prison. He is married to Shirley and they have two daughters.

Once an old lady was going to the doctor. It was pouring with rain and it was a long distance for her to walk from the bus stop. So I drove to the bus station, got the people off and I said to the lady, 'Don't move, I'll make a detour and take you right to the doctor'. She was very happy. I've found children straying early morning because of a family problem and I stop the bus and say, 'Where are you going?' and they tell me they're running away, and I say, 'Come in to the bus' and I take them straight back to their home. You can always make the time up. If I should see you running along the road, waving because you want the bus, I stop. And you say, 'Thank you'. What a nice feeling.

Some time ago I was coming from East Cowes and I got to the bus stop near my house and a chappie said to me, 'There's a fire over there' and I saw it was at the house next to mine. I said to my passengers, 'Just a moment please', and I jumped off the bus, told someone to dial 999, got a ladder from the back of my place, put it by the house on fire, pushed the window up and went right in. Two youngsters were in there and I called to my wife, Shirl, to come, then I took the kids out and passed them over to her and grabbed the mother from the bed, threw a blanket over her – she wasn't dressed, she was asleep – got her out, dashed in the kitchen, got some water and put the fire out. Then I went back to the bus smelling of smoke – I couldn't stop to clean up. The passengers gave me a round of applause and I got a certificate from the Society for the Protection of Life from Fire.

A lot of people ask my advice about their problems and it's not just because I'm a magistrate. My father once told me – if you spit in the sky, it falls on your face. And that's a fact.

The Forest Ranger

This is an ancient hunting forest, 1,180 acres owned by the Forestry Commission, with half coniferous and half deciduous trees. The oldest plantation was started because of the need to have extra timber for boatbuilding in the First World War, and up until thirty-five years ago, we still built fishing smacks on the Island.

Davyd ('Badger') Morgan Moore, 42, was born in Canterbury and has worked in forestry since leaving Edinburgh University twenty-two years ago with a degree in ecology. He came over to the Isle of Wight on holiday in 1990 and never went back. He is now a volunteer ranger at Parkhurst Forest, secretary of the Friends of Parkhurst Forest, and a countryside consultant. He is married to Mandy and they have four young children.

The forest was frequented by Queen Victoria and there's one ride called Queen's Ride. Although paintings and photographs show her as a sour-faced old biddy, this is totally incorrect. She had a great sense of humour. The Queen's Ride got its name from when she was riding through the forest in her open cart, nature called and off she went into the edge of the ride. On coming out, she bumped into one of the forest workers and asked him if the ride had a name. When he said it didn't, she said, 'Well you can call it the Queen's Ride now. I've just christened it'.

We have all manner of people coming here – bikers, horse riders, dog walkers, scenic walkers. The shortest walk is a mile and a quarter, the longest a mile and three-quarters. Some parts can look a little frightening to city dwellers – the trees are so close together and it's very dark inside – but when you get in there and once your eyes get accustomed, there are things you wouldn't see in an open canopy.

One of the biggest problems we've had is with disposable foil barbecues which are brought by countless irresponsible people who either leave them behind or tip the charcoal on the edge of a ride. It doesn't take much of a spark to start a forest fire.

Our local most common, but nationally rare plant is the narrow leaf lungwort – it has a mottled two-tone green elongated leaf and a beautiful array of spiked purple flowers. We have bluebells and primroses open as early as the first week of February. The forest is home to the red squirrel – there are no greys on the Island. The last one tried to come over by the car ferry from Lymington about twelve years ago but we caught him and sent him back. We have nine adult foxes and I've seen seven young cubs so far. We've managed to keep the hunt out because it would damage the ecology. We have a pair of buzzards that fly over and hopefully one day they'll nest here, and there are badgers on the eastern side. There are nightingales, of course, and last night we had a moth hunt and found eighty-one different species. We have thirteen of the fifteen British species of bat here. The night before last, we had over sixty people on a Night Jar and Bat Walk.

We also have glorious wood ants about four times larger than the garden counterpart and if children disturb the nests with a stick, they find the ants do invade parts of their anatomy. They don't bite, but they do squirt a small amount of formic acid, which is very painful. Some of the anthills are about 3 ft high and for every foot above ground, they've got a foot below.

About 5,000 children a year come through the forest, and we go out to schools to give talks. I also do lectures at the Warners' Holiday Centre in Bembridge for visitors who want to know about the Island's ecology. We work closely with Marie and Brian Young (see page 92) who bring their shire horse and cart at week-ends and take people for rides. Going through the forest with a horse and cart is like nothing else. It's so peaceful, just the clip-clop of the horse's hooves. We also use the horses to bring out big timber – they do much less damage than a tractor.

In the main, the forest belongs to the people and we are encouraging them to give us some feedback as to what they'd like. Through the Friends of Parkhurst Forest, we've done a powerful amount of fund-raising and conservation work. By cutting back encroaching growth we've managed to bring out plants that have not reared their heads for the past twenty or thirty years.

We generally have about 3,000 people coming in for our Forest Fair every August. Last year we had a ghoulies and ghosties evening on Halloween. And for the first time last year we had Father Christmas in the forest. We found a little chap – an ex-BT engineer – who really looked the part even without the suit. He had white hair, white beard, bushy eyebrows, little quarter-size glasses on the end of his nose, roly-poly belly and, once we put the suit on, even I began to believe in Father Christmas! We built a log cabin with a decorated tree, a lovely old chair, sacks of presents and candles, and had a horse and cart for candlelit rides round the forest. About 700 people came along without any advertising. It was a frosty night, a full moon, we had a bonfire going and refreshments and I called up each family in turn. What made my evening was when an old gentleman and two old ladies well into their eighties came forward. I looked about and said, 'No children?' 'Oh', one of the ladies said, 'do you have to have children to come and see Santa?' That jolly nearly made me shed tears. It was so fantastic that people of that age should enjoy it so much.

The Harbour Master

Captain Henry Wrigley, 59, came to the Isle of Wight when his father was vicar of Binstead. He went to naval college, was Senior Deck Officer of P & O Orient Lines, worked with the Southampton Harbour Board and at 30 was appointed Harbour Master at Cowes. He is married to Sheila and they have one daughter and twin sons.

Dare I say it, but being at Cowes is almost like running a cruise ship but tied up the whole time. And that's the fun of it. But we're also a busy little commercial harbour with about 1.5 million passengers going through on the ferry service, and over half a million tonnes in total of freight, petroleum, oil, seaborne aggregates and timber coming through the port. Our back-up sailing facilities are an industry vitally important to the economy of the town. I remember at the end of a big international event, one team captain got up and said, 'Where else in the world other than Cowes could you be in a collision in a race and be guaranteed to be back on the starting line the following day because of the excellent back-up facilities on shore?' And that, of course, is where our reputation has grown. But I do look with envy at France where the government has poured money into yachting facilities. Unfortunately, our government hasn't done this and as a result we're struggling hard, but we've come a long way in the last ten years. I take my hat off to the New Zealanders – they've learnt how to televise sailing and bring it into people's homes. As a result they have everyone's interest.

Cowes Week is an incredible regatta. It can be broken down into single-class, deep-keeled cruising-class, and small day-class racing yachts owned by people from all walks of life and in my opinion the backbone of the regatta. This year (1995), we have the royal yacht *Britannia* for a few days which is wonderful and later in the week, the Norwegian and Danish royal yachts.

But not everyone wants to race. The vast majority just enjoy cruising and visiting different places, and one of the nice things about Cowes is that up the river into the Medina Valley away from the busy harbour, the atmosphere changes completely. Folly Reach, for example, is charming, peaceful and quiet, with good facilities for the visitor.

When I first came here thirty-odd years ago, a nice cruising yacht would be towing a dinghy behind it. Not now. They come from marina-type facilities and look for similar facilities when they visit, and that's quite right. Commercial shipping sizes are changing, too, and we have to meet that challenge. We've just produced a harbour plan development which not everyone will agree with, but it is a framework within which we can go forward in the next two or three decades. We're striving to make the harbour safer, provide more facilities and look for growth industries for the future, very important for youngsters growing up here. We're discussing building an outside breakwater, making a dedicated new channel on the other side of the harbour for the new breed of commercial shipping, and trying to separate some of the recreational uses from the commercial ones, because we do pack an awful lot into this harbour.

There are three types of harbours in the UK: those owned by a private company, those owned by local council, and those established by an Act of Parliament as a Harbour Commission. We're a Harbour Commission and have six councillors from the Isle of Wight Council, two from Cowes Town Council, and another eight from traders, commercial shipping and maritime businesses. They meet once a month and also keep an eye on me – a wise thing to do.

We have to pay rental to the Crown Estate Commission, but are financially totally independent. We don't get a penny from the government, or from the council tax. We get harbour dues and mooring fees, and it is these that pay salaries and the maintenance costs of the harbour. A simple dredging contract for, say, £50,000 to £100,000 isn't very much – but where do you get that money from? The cost of keeping a boat at Cowes makes us one of the cheapest harbours on the south coast. This year, it's 18p a foot for a daily visitor; individual mooring in the main harbour is £5.86 per annum, and up river it's cheaper at £4.28 a foot. These prices are from 1 April to the end of October and it's half these rates for the winter period. We are rather proud of the fact that we keep costs down though we do have difficulty in competing with the rest of northern Europe who have different seabed ownerships.

Having been brought up in a vicarage I suppose being a harbour master is almost like being a vicar. You're so involved with people and it covers a host of things. Although we are more a community than a business, in fact, I think we're both. I'm often asked what I do in winter but we're all very busy most of the year, and this is the time we suddenly realize we've got some jolly nice neighbours and friends on the Island.

Most people's image of a harbour master is of an old shellback with grey hair and disgraceful side whiskers, sitting on a bollard chewing tobacco, drinking rum and spinning salty yarns. I've been trying to do this for some time, but I don't think they'll let me.

The Steam Railway Director

I've always been interested in public transport and am fascinated by the unique character of the Isle of Wight railway. The first line between Cowes and Newport opened in 1862 and the line between Ryde and Newport in 1875. These gradually expanded until in 1900 there were 54 miles of railway on the Island. In 1966 Barbara Castle, then Minister of Transport, said the Ryde to Cowes, and Shanklin to Ventnor lines should close, but Ryde to Shanklin be retained. This was electrified and now operates with former London Underground tube trains because they have the right dimensions.

I suppose it was inevitable that when attempts were made to salvage something of the Island's railway industry, I should be a part of it. I've been associated with the steam railway here since its birth in 1971. People from all sorts of jobs came to help at the beginning: bank managers, telephone engineers, some in the insurance world, motor trade, shipping companies. They all had this burning ambition to salvage something before it was lost for ever. But it quickly became apparent we had to operate professionally – there's no leniency just because you're an enthusiast. If you're carrying members of the public everything has to be done properly. There are about sixty volunteers who now work regularly and fulfil operating duties for which they have to be trained and competent. Porters, signalmen, guards, firemen, drivers, platform foremen, booking clerks – it's a constant shuffle on the rota. The youngsters have never seen steam trains, but the enthusiasm is there and we have some who started as schoolboys and are now qualified drivers. We also have a lady fireman, and lady guards.

Jim Loe, 57, is a Londoner and worked for the Commercial Union Assurance Company for thirty-seven years, five of which were in the Isle of Wight. He took early retirement in 1992 and is now the Commercial Director of the Isle of Wight Steam Railway. His partner, Di, is the catering manageress there. He has a daughter from a previous marriage and one granddaughter.

We're restoring Victorian carriages that had been put out to grass as beach huts, holiday homes, even chicken houses. We've already got three into service, one of which dates back to 1864, and there are far more available than we could ever use. The biggest problem is not moving them here, but getting at them over trees and out of people's gardens that weren't there before.

In 1991 we extended the line back $3\frac{1}{2}$ miles to Smallbrook. We laid the track ourselves, but BR made materials available on the mainland, and Wightlink let us bring it all across on the ferry for nothing, lorry load after lorry load. We bought 30,000 tonnes of ballast from north Wales, BR paid to have the £180,000 station built at Smallbrook and the Isle of Wight County Council transferred the leasehold of the land to freehold, so we're now its owners. We're a private limited company and a registered educational charity. The turnover we have comes from our visitors and this has to pay the staff and capital works.

Since 1991 we've been running a 5-mile railway connecting with the Island Line service which runs from Ryde to Shanklin at Smallbrook, and we've re-opened the halt at Ashey. We have five steam locomotives and nine carriages. Our paid staff include the shop manager, chief mechanical engineer, carpenter, joiner, fitter, charge hand, a marketing manager and his assistant, and seasonal staff in the shop and café.

My job is to keep the company solvent and know where we're going to be in ten years' time. But I've also always been interested in the track and still like to work on this, doing fencing and cutting back the banks. I also like to sell tickets, talk to the public, and hear how much they enjoy it all. 'Carry on with the good work, you're doing a super job,' they say. You only have to see the railway when trains are running, and it comes alive. You sense that feeling, the jokes, the friendship, the fun, but also the serious working of what is a proper railway. It's not a toy. It's a proper functioning, living, breathing railway, albeit a museum piece. When people arrive you know full well it's the son or husband who's made the decision for the family to come, and the wife often tells me afterwards that she's said to her husband, 'It's your day, we'll do what you want, we'll go to that railway'. When she gets here, she can see it's not a builder's yard, it's not scruffy, the trains are clean, there's a play area for children, a woodland walk, a museum. One of the first-class carriages that last saw service in 1937 has deep cushioning and antimacassars with lace surrounds on the headrests.

The Steam Train Driver

Ken West, 67, was born on the Isle of Wight and worked for British Rail for fifty years. After the Island's steam train stopped running in 1966 he carried on driving the electric train from Ryde to Shanklin until he retired in 1993. He now works with the Isle of Wight Steam Railway company as a driver and instructor and is married to Margaret who works in the railway's catering department. They have a daughter, who also works for the company, and a son.

After I retired from British Rail, all of a sudden my boyhood love came back and now I'm driving steam trains again. People say, 'Why do you want to do it, if you've done this all your life?' Well, if I didn't like doing it, I wouldn't do it, would I? As soon as I get up in the morning, I stick the old overalls on, get out here, have a laugh and chat. It's a family affair. You respect the management, but we're friends. I've been mentioned in four books about Isle of Wight railway people and I've been on television.

There's not a lot I can do in the workshop here, but I do some shovelling, prepare the engine. If they're a bit short, I come in and do the relief driving. It must be something in the blood. My daughter, she's married and has a beautiful daughter of her own, and she's out here doing a guard's job. Boys still want to be engine drivers, but they don't want to do the work that goes before it. You have to start at rock bottom – there's nothing I couldn't do with that loco No. 24, and the foreman appreciates that. We have a speed limit of 25 miles an hour here, sometimes it's 26, but what you have to look at is, No. 24 was 104 years old on 31 December this year (1995), and you must respect that age and all the hard work that's gone into it. If anything did go wrong and you had a bit of a mishap, there's nothing else to take its place. It's like an old car; if you look after it, it will do the job.

Trains and music – ballads mostly about the old days – are my life really. I used to sing in a choir and I wished I'd kept it going. What's good about living on the Isle of Wight? Well, look at me. I'm 67 and you couldn't get a better man than me, could you?

The Commuter

I moved to the Isle of Wight because the quality of life is better here and the Ryde to Portsmouth catamaran made it possible to travel up to London daily. I get up at 4.30 a.m., feed the cats, make myself a flask of coffee, and sometimes add a tot of whisky. For breakfast I have a yoghurt, grapefruit juice and vitamin pill. I leave home about 5.20 and take my time – it's lovely driving along at that time of day. This week I've seen a fox, a barn owl and a badger. You don't see these in Sidcup. I get the 5.50 catamaran from Ryde, which arrives at Portsmouth Harbour at 6.06. I catch the 6.20 London train and arrive at Waterloo at 7.47. Then it's straight on to the Northern Line to Centre Point at Tottenham Court Road where I work. I'm there by 8 o'clock. I do sleep on the train and that extra hour and a quarter is probably worth three hours at home. I leave my mobile phone on while I'm travelling to do deals with a broker or another bank, and I've got a Reuter's rates machine which tells me all the news alerts and every rate in the world, twenty-four hours a day. I don't talk much on the journey to fellow passengers. We say hello on the ferry and when we're waiting for the train. But the minute we get on it, we all have our separate seats because we need to sleep, and we all understand that.

Coming home, I leave work at 4.30 p.m. providing there are no panics, base rate changes or someone in the world's been assassinated. I catch the 4.50 train, listen to the radio, have a little sleep and I'm home at 7.20 fresher than when I lived in Sidcup and hadn't travelled so far. I don't go to bed until about 11 o'clock, after *News at Ten* and the weather forecast.

I suppose the only stressful part of the travelling is the fare because it's £3,800 a year. It's a lot of money and that's only net. Gross you're probably talking about £5,000. But if you weigh it all up, the money, the travelling time and the quality of life, the latter outweighs everything else.

It used to be great fun at Christmas – British Rail would put on a special carriage for us and we'd have a champagne breakfast on the train. There were about twenty-four to thirty of us then. Now with the recession, or people moving away or retiring, there are probably only six of us left. Really sad.

Richard Overton, 48, started working with the Bank of England when he was 16. After ten years he left to work for a Swiss bank and is now Foreign Exchange Manager of the Commercial Bank of Korea in London. Eighteen years ago, he bought a holiday home at Bembridge on the Isle of Wight, and eleven years ago decided to move with his family from Sidcup, Kent, to live here. He now commutes to London every day. He is Vice-commodore of Brading Haven Yacht Club, will be Commodore in 1996, is a Freeman of the City of London. He is married to Heather and they have two sons.

In some ways we've educated Wightlink about our needs. The ferry used to leave at 6.15 in the morning, but we suggested we would require an earlier one as we wouldn't have got into work until 8.30. They said if we could guarantee thirty passengers on that early morning catamaran, it would pay them to put one on, which they did. And there's never been below that number because it's not just people who travel to London. You've got building workers going to Gosport and Portsmouth.

The weather can be a pain sometimes because the catamarans can be cancelled, but I've never ever in the eleven years I've been travelling every day, not got to work or got home. If the cats (catamarans) don't run, the car ferry takes their place.

I prefer travelling in winter to summer. You get a better sleep for a start, because it's dark in the mornings and evenings, and you haven't got so many holiday-makers. They can be a real pain after a day's work. The climate really is a bit different on the Island. We put coats on when we leave home in the morning, not because we require them here, but because it's a few degrees warmer than the mainland and directly we get to Petersfield, we can feel the change of temperature. It must be one of the nicest lines for scenery in the south-east and now we've got these new trains, there's no need to travel first class.

There are three pluses for living on the Island. They look after old people very well – the doctors are friends rather than someone you just go to see when you're ill; the education is excellent; and I can go to work and know that my wife and family are reasonably safe. You don't drive past when you see someone walking along the road, because you know you're not going to get mugged when you give them a lift. When my wife had a puncture and had to change her tyre on the road, a bus driver got out of his cab and helped her do it.

Since I've been here, I've taught myself to sail and we now have a 24 ft cruiser and four dinghies. I play the tenor sax at the club if people ask me to turn out, I enjoy walking and yacht club activities. And I think the relaxation I get on the train helps me to do my job as a foreign exchange manager which is very stressful. People tell me I look much better than I did when I lived in Sidcup.

The Botanic Gardener

When I came for my interview for the job of curator, and walked round the gardens, they weren't much to look at, but I was overwhelmed by the spirit of the place. The site is a landslip zone, the soil was very impoverished and yet plants do thrive. There used to be a TB hospital here, one of the largest in Europe, and you can feel it's a place of healing.

In the early 1960s when the hospital had closed down, someone with great foresight on Ventnor Urban District Council purchased the site for a public open space and started the gardens. For the next ten years Sir Harold Hillier in Winchester used it for growing plants for his nursery in exchange for supplying the gardens, but when he died the company's benevolence ceased and five years later it was decided to take the gardens out of the Parks Department and put a curator in charge. Which is where I came in.

Because we are virtually frost-free, we can grow a huge range of plants, and we're now developing themes in geographical groupings. As Ventnor was a Victorian/ Edwardian town, we've got a sub-tropical area with plants of that period; we have one of the largest outdoor collections of New Zealand plants in the British Isles; a fairly good Mediterranean collection; and we're working on the American continents and plants from Japan. I've found things grow far better if they're with their own kind. I think they're zenophobic actually!

I have a feeling for things growing among each other, basically a bit of natural 'fighting it out'. In the Mediterranean section, we have genistas and cystus, lavenders and rosemary in a glorious hotch-potch quilt, all flowing into one another. We don't plant in groups of threes and fives, but in forty, fifty, or sixty of any one plant, big bold groupings. And then we'll stick something else in the middle, as you'd find in the wild. We've encouraged an enormous population of birds here: longtail tits, spotted green wood-peckers, jays, buzzards along the cliff edge.

I discuss the garden with my wife, Deb, all the time. We live it and breathe it. We go to bed having talked about it and at 3 o'clock in the morning I get a nudge, and she says, 'I've been thinking, how about if we do such and such. . . .'.

Simon Goodenough, 40, was born in Malta and much of his childhood was spent overseas. He worked with Geests in Spalding, Ealing Parks Department, and at Kew Gardens where he was supervisor of the Temperate and Arboretum Nursery. He became curator of the 23 acre Botanic Gardens near Ventnor in 1986. He is married to Deb, a Canadian, who works in the gardens with him, and they have two young sons.

13

We're probably the most boring people on the face of the earth if you don't like plants. Everywhere we go, we think 'Gosh, we could do that, or use those plants'. We always go on busman's holidays and look at plant associations in the wild, to see if we could ape them. We have about 10,000 species and varieties in the gardens now.

About five years ago we started the Friends of the Gardens and now have around 700 members. We have a seed list each year of about 300 items and they can select 20 packets of their own choice. They also collect and package them and we use the seed to distribute to other gardens. I think more and more people are realizing there is a spiritual need to commune with nature away from computers and cellnet phones. Our association with plants is a deep-seated thing. If it wasn't for them we wouldn't be here – everything we wear has plant connections: the table we're sitting at, beer, even meat products. Most of our medicines originally came from plants. I have this argument with my pharmacist friends – their conventional medicine is only 100 years old. It's not medicine at all. It's biochemistry. People lose sight of this.

My favourite part of the gardens is the nursery where things germinate. It's the engine-room with these little packets of seeds coming from all over the world, and those who work there are nurturing this miracle that 300,000 people enjoy every year.

I fear sometimes the gardens are seen as just another tourist attraction and not for what they are, which is a spiritual haven. We do fall flat on our faces from time to time, but we're pushing the bounds of what can and can't be done in a British garden. It's free to come in, except for the car park and long may it remain so. We need financial assistance to keep the thing going, but it's so important for the well-being of society to have something like this to escape the madding crowd.

The Vicar

When I first started training for the Ministry, it was a controversial thing to do, but not publicly so. My training was exactly the same as a male priest would have had, but as women weren't able to be ordained, I became a deaconess. I was among the first women in the Portsmouth diocese to be made priests, and the first woman to be appointed rector. Someone described it beautifully when they said, 'Well, our Sandra's historic'. And of course it *is* making history.

I didn't have any illusions that it wouldn't be difficult. But I believed I'd been given a sense of vocation to the priesthood and had to allow the Church to test it, which it did. It was a bit of a surprise to find myself involved in something that was making headlines, because one of my better characteristics is that I'm ordinary. Although it was controversial, it was also new and exciting, and at the same time there was a feeling it was quite normal, because it was right for me.

I knew one would have to go very gently with people because it was going to be a new experience for them. Most took the attitude, 'Well, we're not too sure about having a woman in a dog collar around, but we'll see how it works out'. Now I have the security of the job, and people have the security of knowing I'm here as their priest.

There have been two people in our parish whose churchmanship has made it impossible to accept a woman priest and they usually go to a neighbouring church. I don't think there's been much against me on a personal level – at least I hope there hasn't. It's difficult because I don't like being a source of sadness, or feeling I've been responsible for someone choosing to move church. But I have to balance that with the overwhelming support from others, and the parishes were very carefully listened to before the appointment was made. On the Sunday following my ordination as a priest in Portsmouth Cathedral, I celebrated communion service here in the village church at Niton for the first time and we lost count at over 250 people who'd come because they wanted to share that moment. It was a very, very special day.

We have Sunday services in each of the three parishes but there is lay help and also a retired priest. I use a bicycle – I don't drive – and this means I am visible, that I can stop and talk. I think village communities do appreciate seeing the vicar around – rather like seeing the policeman.

In a village you have to deal with everything. Life is not protected here, and because you know people, you're taken

The Revd Sandra Lloyd, 47, was born in the West Midlands and lived there for twenty-two years before moving to Hertfordshire and, eighteen years ago to the Isle of Wight when her husband, Malcolm, began work at County Hall. They have two grown-up children. About thirteen years ago she started a three-year training for the Ministry. She served her first curacy at Freshwater, was appointed curate to the parishes of Whitwell, St Lawrence and Niton, and in January 1995, became their incumbent, the only woman incumbent in the Portsmouth diocese.

into their lives in perhaps a deeper way, especially at significant moments. But it's also difficult to have strong friendships because those could be misinterpreted and you can't take the attitude of being a friend to everybody, because there's a touch of being false about it. But I try to be available, approachable and so much a part of village life that people forget I'm the vicar and come as a friend.

I'm aware sometimes that people who encounter a woman taking a service for the first time are thinking: my goodness, will it be alright? It's often at funerals where this happens. I hope at the end of it they'll be able to say, 'Yes, that was good, a woman's touch worth having'. They can also be a bit surprised to find an ordinary, nearly middle-aged mum who really doesn't fit any of the pre-conceived notions of what it's like to be a clergy person. But I think there are times, often at a bereavement, when being a woman does help. People have said to me, 'Well, I can cry with you. If it had been a man I would have kept a stiff upper lip'. And sometimes at christenings, they say I know how to hold the baby!

With regard to clothes, men priests mostly wear darker colours, but I'm first and foremost a woman and know what I feel comfortable in. I used to wear a lot of frilly necked blouses and if you cut an inch off the bottom, you can make a channel for a clerical collar! But now clerical outfitters have realized there are a lot of women priests and deacons, and you can get a huge variety of colours and patterns. I've also got the equivalent of the executive's power suit – a very feminine black suit for the occasions when dark colours are more appropriate.

My family have always been very supportive and I couldn't have done it if they hadn't been. I think they've enjoyed seeing Mum develop as a person. My husband doesn't say much, but he beams! At times it is difficult to be the vicar's spouse, because there's no role model, but he's learnt to cook and do Sunday lunch because he rapidly realized it would be bread and cheese otherwise! And my daughter, Cariad, has been my unpaid telephone lady for years because people come and ask for help, and she copes beautifully.

This village had been eighteen months without its own vicar before me, and when we came here, someone who doesn't come to church remarked, 'It's good to know there are lights on in the rectory and people are living there – the village feels alright now'. I think they were actually meaning: if you haven't got a clergy person there, the heart of the village is missing. But I still haven't got that person to come to church!

The Builder

Anthony Caws, my great-great-grandfather, built Seaview Hotel and eight houses down the same road for his eight children. When the press gang in the Napoleonic Wars came to get him from his home in Rose Cottage, he hid by climbing into a big bed with his children and they didn't find him. After that he built a priest's hole in the floor. About twenty years ago I was renovating Rose Cottage, as it's still called, and when we took the floor up, I found the old priest's hole, so I knew exactly what it was.

Will Caws, 52, has lived in Seaview all his life, as his family has done since 1680. Before setting up his own building company (Caws and Hermans) with Rob Hermans, he worked in a shipyard in Cowes, for a traditional boatbuilder and a house builder. He is married to Mary and they have four daughters. Caws is one of the oldest Island names and the family crest reads: Faithful to God and King.

There used to be a big suspension pier in Seaview and Frank Caws, my great-uncle, was the structural engineer. It was built about 1860 and blew down in a storm in 1951. There are lots of bits of it in Seaview houses, pitch pine doesn't rot. It was a beautiful pier and I remember as a child seeing the pilot boat come in there. There's been a regatta here every August for many, many years, and it has stayed totally as it was. I always feel if my great-grandfather came back on that day, he would recognize it immediately. There's sailing for two days, sports like the old egg and spoon race, high jump, tug of war, greasy pole, swimming, diving, a big rowing event (I've rowed in it for forty-three years and always won a cup of some kind) and a grand display of fireworks at the end.

If you live in Seaview for a while, you don't want to leave it. I nearly emigrated to Australia when I was young because I couldn't find enough work, but then people started asking me to put roofs on their houses, and I thought I'd not make any more money out there, so I stayed. That's how I started in business with Rob my partner, twenty-five years ago. We employ eighteen guys now and all our work is here in Seaview.

The village is not like a lot of others where townies have bought up houses and ruined the place. This village has always been a second home for a lot of people, and many old families like the Garnetts, Holbrooks, Simmonds and Dobbs have been coming here for generations. So, although they don't necessarily live here full-time, they are part of the village. The shops make their money in summer and tick over in winter. My brother owns the shoe shop, the fourth generation of our family to be in the business, and if you think of any shops that shouldn't survive in a village this size, it's a shoe shop. Yet it's probably one of the healthiest businesses – Jim never says he hasn't got something. He'll either have it or will get it for you.

The village has a snooty reputation? Well, yes, but we sort them out! In the old days we used to fight with the yachties and only a few years ago, the yacht club was still absolutely taboo to the locals even though my family used to own it. They would have kicked me out if I'd gone there. It was them and us, and we were called those horrible village boys. But that's all come to an end. It changed in the 1980s, and we're all members of the club now.

From May to September I never leave the Island unless I have to. In the winter I go to London and I do have good holidays. But I'm never happier than when I'm back on that boat coming home. I always feel that here I can go somewhere and know my great-great-grandfather has walked that way too; it's a sort of *déjà vu* feeling. I believe that not only can genes be passed down, so you look like your father or grandfather, but thoughts and memories too. This happens to me quite a lot and I think it's the reason why.

The Lifeboat Man

I'd been involved in a lifeboat project to raise money for an in-shore lifeboat in Lewes, so when I came to a place where there was a lifeboat station, it was an automatic thing to ask David Kennett, the coxswain, if I could be involved even though I'd never been to sea in my life. He said, 'Come along 10 o'clock Sunday morning and we'll start you off. If you don't fit in, I'll tell you'. He was quite honest and open about it.

There are two RNLI lifeboat stations on the Island – at Yarmouth and Bembridge – and other stations around the Island run by people involved in in-shore rescue.

We have about twenty-three crew members at Yarmouth and need seven on a 'shout', so there's quite fierce competition for places on the boat. But the large number we have gives us coverage for holidays, days off, and other things. I can remember ten years ago, we were down to about ten, and that meant you couldn't really leave town. We have a tremendous cross-section of people: the coxswain owns a boatyard, there are two artists, a sheet metal worker, prison officer, electrician, printer. . . .

The in-shore boat can only go out in certain conditions, whereas we have an all-weather boat – an Arun Class lifeboat, about 18 years old and a superb seaboat. We even went out in the 1987 hurricane which was quite lively. It can take us across to France though our patch is roughly from Cowes to Bournemouth. We average between forty and forty-five calls a year, from boats on fire to towing boats in danger of being mowed down by shipping. We deal with death, of course, and you become familiar with it. The best thing to do is to get back out in the boat again. There's a lot of gallows humour, but that's just a mask covering your own fear.

There was a chap who was a great friend of a lot of people, myself included. He was out in a speedboat, and there was a tug and a barge under tow. The speedboat hit the tow-line, he didn't see it, it wasn't lit, and he was all but decapitated. We spent all night in a search for a girl who'd been on the boat with him, looking for her in the water with flares, but we didn't find her. They're the bad ones. When you know someone is in the water, and you should find them and don't. You live with these regrets almost more than the deaths, strangely enough.

The satisfaction of a good job done is unbelievable. The best one I've had was very close to Yarmouth. We were painting the lifeboat house and our local doctor was with us when the coastguard rang and said 'immediate launch'. It was to go to a yacht about 2 miles east of Yarmouth, on board which was a baby, who had had some kind of fit and stopped breathing, although the parents had revived the infant. We left the harbour ever so

Paul McKillop, 43, was born in Glasgow and studied electronics at Glasgow University. He installed computers for United Biscuits and worked as manager of the White Hart Hotel in Lewes, Sussex, before, fourteen years ago, becoming manager of Holdings bookshop in Yarmouth on the Isle of Wight. He is separated from his wife and has two children.

quickly, we were doing nearly 15 knots because we knew the urgency. We got to the boat, and I'll never forget the mother handing me her child – you could see the mixture of emotions on her face. I took the baby into the doctor, who had set up an operating table. He treated the baby, who we then took back to Yarmouth and put into a waiting ambulance. The whole thing took seventeen minutes.

At 4 o'clock on a winter's night, with a gale blowing up, you think why am I doing this job? But then a good rescue reassures you that it is all worthwhile. What we get concerned about is when a casualty overstates his danger to the coastguard, and his difficulty could be dealt with by a commercial tow. If *we* go to him, say he's 10 miles south of The Needles, we're then not in a position to help if someone needs us urgently 200 yards off Yarmouth pier.

There is a tremendous buzz about being in the lifeboat, and great comradeship. The crew don't just work together on the boat, we socialize together too. People who don't fit in, drop out. It happens without anybody saying anything. They come along and find they don't like it, or perhaps families don't like it. A lifeboat man needs tremendous support from his family because the consequences of the maroon going off rattle down the community.

Here in the shop, I dash off and Betty, the book buyer, has to make sure that if I'm not back before closing time, the keys are left for me somewhere safe. Families have ruined lunches, a planned visit somewhere with the children has to be called off suddenly without warning. They quickly come to accept it, but it can be stressful on a marriage.

We can get rough seas here, we've had big ones with up to 30 ft waves, but that's rare. We can have a short and uncomfortable sea. The Arun will go up on a wave and fall off the top and come slamming down – it's the best roller-coaster in the world. You don't have to be fit in the way of being able to hump heavy weights around, but you do have to have a lot of determination and staying power. I'm still sick when it's very rough, but you just have to carry on with the job. I think there are only two or three on the boat who aren't the same.

The Lighthouse Keeper

This lighthouse was first switched on, on 25 March 1840. It is 89 ft high and is now the only manned one on the Island, though there is one on each corner – The Needles on the west coast, The Nab Tower to the east, and a small beacon on the most northerly point, now discontinued. The main navigation light to warn shipping here at the southern tip of the Isle of Wight has a range of 30 miles, and 15 ft below it there's a red light to warn about a reef of rocks, Atherfield Ledge, out to the west of us.

The Needles was automated at the end of last year (1994) in a blaze of publicity – nobody wanted the crews to come off – but it's now controlled from Harwich, as this one will be in two years' time. There's now only one manned off-shore lighthouse in Britain and that's in the Channel Islands. By the turn of the century, there will be none left and the job of lighthouse keeper will cease to exist. It's sad really. With technology the way it is, they can monitor lighthouses quite successfully, but you're taking away the human element, and today there are more people spending more time at sea and less people to look after them. The government has decimated the coastguard service, and now they're decimating us as well.

Here at St Catherine's there's a family still living in the house beneath the base of the tower, and the rest of the accommodation is for relief quarters and a holiday house for Trinity House personnel. I lived there until two years ago. It was very nice – the house is double-glazed and centrally heated and you don't pay mortgage or electricity bills. It's quite a shock when you come out into the real world.

During the summer season we have holiday-makers round here most of the time, but during the winter you can have an eight-hour shift and not see or hear from a soul. You get used to it, but sometimes it gets a bit boring. Until recently, we were controlling lighthouses from here right the way down to Cornwall, but our computers have now been withdrawn and there's central monitoring at Harwich. All we've got left is the office computer, and one to monitor the Decca navigation system. And all we have to do with that, is push a button once an hour and look at the screen to make sure it's behaving itself.

Ralph Humphries, 44, was born on the Isle of Wight. He trained as an apprentice motor mechanic, and applied to work on a Trinity House ship. There were no vacancies and he was told if he went to a lighthouse, he'd be transferred in three months' time. Twenty-four years later, he says, he is still waiting for his transfer. He has worked in thirty-four lighthouses around the UK coast and is now principal keeper at St Catherine's Lighthouse. He is separated from his wife and has two children.

The lighthouse is open in the summer months but not all keepers will take people round because we are personally responsible for them while they're on the station. And we get clobbered for tax – if people put a donation in the hat, you have to declare it. Women lighthouse keepers? When they brought in equal rights for women, we were one of the exemptions because they thought two women and one man on an off-shore lighthouse might not go down too well, and that three men would get on better than three women would!

We have two crews of three here, and we work a twenty-eight day tour of duty alternating with another crew. But you also have to be on stand-by so if someone goes sick, you can be called in to take over. We do weather reports for the Met. Office every hour, twenty-four hours a day, and reports every four hours for Trinity House, the coastguards and anyone who wants to call us up. We quite often get calls from pigeon fanciers wanting to know which way the wind's blowing and how high the cloud is so the pigeons don't get lost.

We have to give our first weather report at 4.45 in the morning, so I get here in time to make a cup of tea and start cleaning the place down before that. As principal keeper, I do all the book work as well.

For the weather report, you start off with the temperature, then take wind direction and speed, and pressure from the barometer. Visibility is purely by eyesight: if you can see the Dorset coast, that's 29 miles away; The Needles Lighthouse is 15 miles; the rest is pure educated guesswork. You note the type of cloud, how much and how high it is, and that's educated guesswork too. At night we have a searchlight which sends a beam on to the cloud, and wherever it hits it, we use an alidade to measure off the angle. We record the maximum and minimum amount of rain, any thunderstorms, hail or sleet. We get the shipping forecast twice a day from BT ship-to-shore radio stations.

Most people are very impressed by the cleanliness here. It's not just clean, it's sparkling clean, and the lens for the main navigation light is absolutely spotless. This gets cleaned every day and washed and polished once a week as well. I've been in lighthouses for twenty-four years and this still never fails to amaze me. Once a week, whoever happens to be on duty will sweep and wash the tower down from top to bottom, which is about an hour and a half's work. With the amount of salt spray coming over here, the windows are a never-ending job. We still get inspected once a year – in the old days the inspectors were ex-Royal or Merchant Navy captains and some of them used to wear white gloves with which they would very deliberately rub their fingers across something to see if it was as polished as it should be. They're not as bad as that now, but they still come in and their assessment of the principal keeper is made from these visits as well.

There's a journal in the lighthouse tower which dates from 1943 and on 1 June that year at 11 o'clock, the lighthouse was bombed; the three keepers ran into the engine-room to be safe, but that took a direct hit and all were killed. They're buried in a mass grave up in Niton. The lighthouse was re-manned and operational again by that evening.

The Coastguard

The UK coast is divided into six regions, within each region there's a district, and in each district a number of sectors. Emergency calls go to Lee-on-Solent and are farmed out to people like myself for local co-ordination – they can't see what's going on south of The Needles.

I have about forty auxiliary coastguards – all part-time volunteers – at Bembridge, Ventnor, and The Needles, with small teams at Ryde and Newport where they man the landing site for a helicopter that can take people to hospital. Each station is equipped with a vehicle that carries cliff rescue and beach-searching equipment, and at week-ends and holidays the auxiliaries are out keeping a watch and doing general PR duties. We go to local fêtes and attend anything that's marine-oriented. It's good for people on the Island to know we're still here. Auxiliaries are paid, though not very well, for their training and duties and for attending incidents. But they do a lot on a voluntary basis as well.

Their training covers a whole range of things from vehicle driving to recognition of vessels and navigation. I find out first if they can swim – it's not essential, but

John Trill, 53, was born in Winchelsea, Sussex, served in the Royal Navy for twelve years, and joined the coastguard in 1972. He worked in Aldeburgh and Dover before coming to the Isle of Wight. He is the only full-time professional coastguard on the Island, and is responsible to the district controller at Lee-on-Solent. He is married to Valerie and they have two children.

better if they can – and if they're afraid of heights. In the training, we put them over a cliff with all the gear, then recover them with the stretchers and dummies. I don't insist everyone goes down, and in each team of ten there are probably no more than one or two who would rather not do this. Strength isn't always necessary for cliff rescues. One of our auxiliaries is a very tiny woman – you'd think a good wind could blow her away – but she goes up and down with no problems and as long as they can hold on to and secure the person or animal that's fallen, that's half the task done because we use a winch to bring them back.

The main thing an auxiliary needs is commonsense and enthusiasm. There are times when they'll be on their own and I can't train them for every eventuality. There are also times when they go for long periods without doing anything. It's quite hard to maintain their enthusiasm if they keep training and never put it to use. So they do need a sense of loyalty and commitment. But this year, we've done something like twenty-eight cliff rescues – I always work on the assumption that if someone's dog goes over the cliff, we need to go and get the dog back or the owner will go over the top as well.

Most coastguards do the job because they like working for the local community – there's still a lot of that kind of feeling about. I've got quite a long waiting list of people wanting to join and at the moment I'm asking some of the older ones to go so I can bring younger ones in. It's been getting to the stage when they're all 35 to 40+ and you really do need younger ones to come through.

One of the worst days I can remember was on an August Bank Holiday a few years ago. It started off nice and calm, but by about 2 o'clock in the afternoon a very strong storm came in from the south-west and we probably dealt with thirty or forty incidents in four or five hours. There's a shingle bank that runs all the way down through here which marks the entrance to The Needles passage. Two or three boats hit this and it was end over end. I think four people from two yachts died. They should, of course, have known better than to be where they were, but they were there and we had to help them the best we could. The trouble is that today anyone can buy a boat and the following day set out to sea without knowing anything about how to sail.

But we've had some good experiences too. There was a 6-year-old lad with apparently a mental age of 2 or 3. His parents were sitting on the beach by Shanklin pier, took their eyes off him for a moment, and he disappeared. About four hours later we were still searching for him, and eventually got the helicopter out. They found him 3 or 4 miles away sitting on a rock surrounded by water, hoisted him off and brought him back. How he got there, we just don't know.

The Diver

I was always fascinated by what was underwater, snorkelling around, pulling up bits and pieces, and I got a job that combined diving and navigation. It was easy to go from that into the oil industry as a diver, though in those early days of North Sea oil there were terrible accidents – we all lost a lot of friends.

And then we got into space age technology, what they call saturation diving, where several people live for a month in a 10 ft by 7 ft chamber on the ship with a gas pressure equivalent to the seabed depth. From this, you commute back and forth in a diving belt until you reach the same pressure on the seabed. It was very lucrative and a means to do other things like wreck and salvage work. This is a very speculative business and not many people survive in it, so you have to have something behind you to absorb the time when you're not earning any money.

I'd had the idea of opening a shipwreck and maritime museum for years because I couldn't bear to part with all the things I'd found on the wrecks – they were part of local history. So when an old bakery in Bembridge, where I'd once been a baker's boy, came up for sale, we bought it and converted it to a museum. It now has all the stuff I've found over the years. Probably the best thing I discovered was the wreck of the submarine *Swordfish* from the Second World War because it was totally unexpected. It was supposed to have been on the west coast of France. It had suddenly disappeared with all the crew and was never seen

Martin Woodward, 46, came to live in Bembridge from Southsea when he was 10. He trained as a navigator at the King Edward VII Nautical College, went into the Merchant Navy on tramp ships in the mid-1960s and in 1968 joined the diving industry. He has since worked as a consultant and commercial diver in various parts of the world, recently in Vietnam, Thailand, Hong Kong and Florida. He is the coxswain of the Bembridge lifeboat, has written a book, *Bembridge 1880 to 1930*, and in the late 1970s started the Shipwreck Centre and Maritime Museum at Bembridge, which his wife Katherine now runs. They have a 3-year-old daughter, and he has a 25-year-old daughter from a previous marriage.

again. I discovered it about twelve years ago now, and it created quite a stir. I've brought up scores of items and the history of each one means so much to me that I remember everything about it. Portholes are just standard ships fittings, but I can go into the museum and remember which porthole came from which ship.

I sometimes buy modern wrecks and if anyone gets too ostentatious at a party and asks me what I do, I say I'm a ship owner, and then list off all these ships I own. About half an hour later, I tell them they're piles of metal on the seabed!

The oldest wreck I've found probably dates from the fifteenth century, but a couple of years ago I did find a third-century Roman gold aureus (coin), and that was beautiful. I hate the word treasure hunter because I'm not motivated by things like gold coins. They're nice to find, but it's the personal thing that was someone's property that appeals to me, like the 200-year-old folding boxwood carpenter's ruler from an old East Indian wreck, and a little bronze cannon, about 3 in long, made 300 years ago. Someone must have made a model of the ship they were on, and there it was with the little hand-made bronze cannon to go with it. It's not worth very much, of course, but it was a lovely find. In fact, I've now found eighteen of them.

When I first started working on wrecks, you just dropped over the side and swam around until you found something. Now I have a specially designed boat with sonars and underwater metal detectors that can cover a sweep of 150 m on each side of the boat. You may have flat calm on the surface, but it will be absolutely black underwater, and no visibility. There are still a lot of hurdles to overcome.

The most enjoyable part of the work is finding something no one else has ever found. You're in a time capsule, and you know you're the first person to touch something from however long ago it is. Even after 150 uncharted wrecks, I still get the same buzz when I find another one.

The Commodore

I think they must have been very desperate when they asked me to be Rear Commodore. Bembridge is fairly old-fashioned, and women don't come first or equal or anything. They first asked me about six years ago at a time when the harbour was owned by a Dutch company and we didn't know if the club was going to stay here. The club-house was originally a cricket pavilion erected here in 1886, and in the bar we have wonderful photographs of regatta days from that time, with ladies in crinolines, huge hats and parasols. By the 1990s nobody for years had been able to do much in the way of repairs or decoration and it had got to the stage where you didn't bring your friends to the club for lunch because it was uncomfortable to say the least. When the wind blew in the library you could hardly hear yourself speak. Now it's a lovely room. I was incredibly lucky because any woman likes making a home and I managed to persuade those in control to give me some money to turn the club into a place you could be proud of. And now the members are.

The club is run by a management committee and flag officers, with a commodore, vice-commodore and two rear commodores. It was Lord Gainsborough, the previous commodore, who asked me if I'd take on the job. I said, 'Well, I'm no good at sitting at the head of a table as chairman and doing nothing.' He said he'd take that on board and told me, 'You can speculate to accumulate but if it doesn't go well, you're out'. Bembridge is not a place that takes kindly to females. On the other hand as they have a slightly Victorian attitude, they found it hard to say no to me.

We have nearly 900 members now. They can join at the age of six as Junior Cadets and go out in little dinghies. They don't have to sail at all at that age, but we make them cadets so we can have them looked after. In the Victorian days when the club started, children were all tucked away at home or were on the beaches with nannies. Nowadays, people haven't got nannies, so we must make children welcome. I think Bembridge has some of the best sailing and racing water in the Island because there's a far less difficult tide and you can learn to become a good helmsman more easily than at Cowes. Some members are now fourth and fifth generations.

A lot of yacht clubs are rather staid and a bit pompous but my way of doing things is to build up a happy family home because I think that's what holidays are about. I've made certain the garden has pretty flowers, and we put in

Penelope ('Pepe') Stratton, 64, was born in Berkshire and her family had a holiday cottage in St Helens, a converted railway station they bought in 1956, two years after it was closed down. It is here that she and her husband, Vernon, now live. Both have always been keen sailors and were chosen for Olympic sailing trials in 1952. Pepe did secretarial work before she married, and subsequently worked for the Girl Guides. She is now Commodore of the 110-year-old Bembridge Sailing Club, the first woman to hold the position. She has four children and nine grandchildren.

chess and backgammon for the children. One of the things I started was *The Pepe Prattle*, a newsletter telling members what's going on. I also thought it would be a good idea to get advertisements for our Year Book, and these now not only pay for the book but bring in a bit more money as well. I asked all the advertisers in for a drink after Christmas to give them their books, so the village and the Island people came into the club. Quite a lot had never been before, and that was the atmosphere to break down.

I think most of the world would tell you Bembridge is the most stuffy, snobby club. In actual fact, anyone who comes to visit it, says how warm and welcoming it is. We do have quite a high subscription because you have to make your money from just two months of the year, in the summer holidays. There is a lot of activity in the winter with retired people, but they are not the ones who spend the big money.

I'll be retiring at the next AGM. I think I want to. It's a funny thing. People get used to you and I can see exactly what happened to Maggie Thatcher. You begin to think you know what's best and you don't. You've probably used up most of your ideas and need to be sorted out. I sit here with the chairmen of banks, accountancy firms and city businesses and stockbrokers, and say, 'Come on gentlemen, you've got to make up your minds. We've been here an hour already, do you want to be here all the afternoon?' What do they say? 'Yes, Pepe' but they do make good decisions for the club.

People always think the Isle of Wight is OAPs and buckets and spades. In fact it's a magical place but the world doesn't know it. I could use a word that's totally abused to describe it. It's 'nice'. There isn't the graft, it doesn't matter what your walk of life is, people value the right things. Yes, of course, you get those who abuse it – I'm not saying all Islanders are good. And if I say it's more like fifty years ago, I don't mean it's out of date, but that the standards and values are more like fifty years ago. You can wake up in the morning, go for a walk on the beach, the sun's shining, the moored boats are waiting to go to Portsmouth, and you feel there's nowhere else in the world you'd rather be. The world is in sight, but it somehow or other isn't going to harm you.

The Race Organizer

The Island Sailing Club is one of five such clubs in Cowes: the Royal Yacht Squadron, Royal London, Royal Corinthian, and Cowes Corinthian. The Royal Yacht Squadron is very select and you have to be invited to join. It's said there are well-known people who applied and weren't able to – I think the most famous was Tommy Lipton who ran Lipton's grocery chain and owned many yachts which tried to wrest the America's Cup back from the USA. But because he was described as a tradesman, they wouldn't let him in! They still have a separate entrance for women and we're told Queen Victoria wasn't able to enter and that's why the Royal Victoria Yacht Club in Ryde was founded. The Island Sailing Club is very cosmopolitan. We have about 2,500 members and are one of the biggest in the country, though two-thirds are from the mainland.

Tony Pearson, 64, was born in London, joined the Navy in 1949, became a pilot, was stationed in America and Greece, and served as a captain of a minesweeper in Scotland. He was involved in Korean and Malaysian wars and in the first Iraq/Kuwait confrontation. He retired in 1981, worked with an electronic group for five years, became bursar of a south London school and then came to live in the Isle of Wight where his family have had a holiday house since the last century. In 1988 he became Secretary of the Island Sailing Club and now organizes the annual Round the Island Race, held each June. He is married to Jane and they have four sons.

The first Round the Island Race was held in 1931 and we're having the sixtieth next year (1996). It was the brainchild of a Major Windeler, a member of this club. In the first year, twenty-five boats took part. This year we had just on 1,300. The record is 1,813 in 1989. The race is about 50 sea miles long, and the multi-hull record is the fastest so far – 3 hours 55 minutes. The mono-hull record was 5 hours 35 minutes and 18 seconds. If the weather is going to be bad, we don't let the smaller boats go out, and if it's very bad we'd postpone it, but we've never had to do that yet.

Although some boats can get round in three or four hours, a number of slow old ones may take twelve or more, and there has to be time in low wind conditions for the slowest of all the eight classes to get way down to The Needles before the tide turns against them, or at least to The Narrows at Hurst Castle where the tide runs very strongly. The minimum sized boat must be 16 ft water line length and over 1,700 lb weight, but there's no limit to the largest. We police the race ourselves with four fast rigid inflatables that whizz around with our race marshals on board. It all works pretty well.

We have a very close liaison with harbour masters in Southampton, Cowes and Portsmouth who control this area and although they can't stop an 80,000 ton container vessel coming down this part of the Solent and going right through the line of small boats – we actually had the *Queen Elizabeth* through at the last race – they can control their speed so they can slip in through the ten minute slot between the classes.

There are accidents. There's a ledge at The Needles which is a hazard for yachts: two big ones went on to it this year, were damaged and the crew had to be taken off. We've produced a safety leaflet on how to avoid the ledge, but highly competitive yachtsmen all take a chance, and in almost every race someone takes a risk and loses.

When Major Windeler first wanted to give a trophy to the winner, he liked the design of a Roman chalice cup that had just been found in the Thames. A replica was made in silver gilt, but he said nothing but the best was good enough for the Round the Island Race, and had another made in solid gold. This is now the most prestigious of the fifty-seven major trophies to be won. Because the race is on handicap, you sometimes get quite a small boat winning. Last year (1994), a small Folk boat, produced before the war, won against expensive and highly-tuned 60 ft racing yachts.

The race is a terrific spectacle. You have streams of boats going off down the western Solent, streams coming up from the east, and all converging into the central Solent for their start times. Then they're off, beating down the Channel, converging on Yarmouth, going through The Narrows, round The Needles and, if there's a prevailing westerly, that's where they're all hoisting their multi-coloured spinnakers and you see this riot of colour going down the back of the Wight.

We have 140 volunteers keeping track of where the yachts have got to, and manning radio stations. The chief racing officer is in race control, where I sit trying to patch things up or sort out anything that's gone wrong. We have about fifteen operators in the library taking people's arrival times as they cross the line, from three vessels moored in the Solent. We aim to have the result of a boat on the electronic display screens within ten minutes of its finishing. The record is two minutes.

The Cruise Boat Administrator

We have three boats at Cowes, one at Ryde, one at Poole, and we're the only cruise boat company on the Island, excluding the ferries. We started about 1973 – those were in the days when we could take all three boats down to West Cowes and have a queue waiting to go out on them. Unfortunately times have changed; there isn't the money around now. But it's no good just sitting here, we have to go out and get customers. We have three staff who go round and give talks at holiday camps and on coaches.

I work on the administrative side of the business. Mark does the mechanics and crewing and he's built all the boats. We run pleasure cruises, theatre trips to Southampton, boat and coach trips to Chessington and Thorpe Park. We've done a commuter run from the Island for ten years now for early morning workmen, and have also had some really lovely wedding receptions on our big boat which can take 500 people.

Jenny Rayment, 45, was born near Basingstoke and moved to the Isle of Wight when she was 5. After school she worked in a jeweller's shop. She is married to Mark and they own three companies: Solent Cruises, Wight Line Cruises and Blue Funnel Cruises in Poole. Their son Lee, 22, manages the business at Poole, and they have a daughter Alison, 19.

We're the Island ambulance and can whip a patient to Southampton or Portsmouth if there's an emergency and they can't get a helicopter. One day Mark was on Cowes Parade and a lady came along with a little boy in a pushchair and said, 'I'd like to thank you. Look at him now'. Mark didn't have a clue what she was talking about. But she told him a few months ago he'd taken her and her little boy over to the mainland in the middle of the night and it was touch and go if the child would be alright. 'But,' she said, 'he's ever so healthy now.' That was quite nice.

We work a twenty-four hour service for the ambulance, but aren't so pleased to hear from grotty yachties who ring up in the middle of the night in Cowes Week asking for a boat to go back to the mainland because they've missed the last ferry. But I love the Cowes Week fireworks and we never have to advertise for that night. We use every single boat we've got, it's worse than a London traffic jam. There's the most fantastic display and to see all the other boats with their lights on, it's beautiful. Everybody is friendly, they shout and talk to each other. Sometimes the *Britannia* moors off Cowes, and the British do love their royalty. To see Prince Philip, Prince Andrew or Princess

Ann step off at the Royal Yacht Squadron steps is a delight. Customers love it and I'm a definite royalist.

Ambitions? I think to carry on as we are for as long as we can. Mark's the ambitious one. I'm just the one that plods on behind and says, 'Oh no, not another boat'!

The Ferry Captain

Brian Bowers, 59, comes from Gosport. He went to sea at 16 with BP Tankers, worked with Blue Funnel Line and went to the Far East, and with Palm Lines travelling to West Africa until the Nigerian civil war ended that trade. He joined the Isle of Wight ferries in 1967, and came to live on the Island in 1976. He is now a captain on the Wightlink ferry boats, is married to Elizabeth and they have three daughters.

The ferries to the Isle of Wight have become very competitive. Wightlink run car ferries from Portsmouth to Fishbourne, catamarans from Portsmouth to Ryde pier, and car and passenger ferries from Lymington to Yarmouth. Red Funnel have car ferries from Southampton to East Cowes, and fast ferries from Southampton to West Cowes. The other competitor is the hovercraft which goes from Southsea to Ryde.

At present Wightlink have a more frequent service and we run all night. Red Funnel run up to midnight and start again at 4 o'clock in the morning. To Islanders this is very important. Someone gets into Gatwick at one in the morning, and at least they can still get home. The only problem on our car ferries is that foot passengers have to come on and off the same time as the cars and if it's raining, they're stuck out in the wet. That's where Red Funnel score over us; they have a separate gangway for foot passengers as indeed Lymington does.

Wightlink was originally part of Sealink but is now owned by a Mr Aiken and a Mr Mulvey. The first thing they did was to smarten us all up, which was good. All the officers wear a cap now, everyone wears a uniform. We're waiting to see what else they'll do.

In the last two years Red Funnel have had new ships and almost doubled their capacity for passengers, threatening us all round with prices and services. So that's sharpening us up and must be good for the Islanders. The fares have come down and if regular passengers buy 100 tickets, they travel at half price. The traditional fortnight's holiday on the Island has changed a lot. People now come for short periods and many families for a second holiday. We've had a lot of day-trippers this year – it's £32 for a car and four people. We are getting the quantity of people, but not the same revenue.

Local people used to say that having everything come by boat added to the cost of living here, but since the multiple stores have arrived, I would think the cost has been reduced. When we first came in 1976, we were certainly paying 10p a gallon more for petrol. Now it's the same as the mainland in some petrol stations.

This is a very busy stretch of water. It's tricky too. Big ships can be avoided because we know where the deep water is that they use. But yachts are more of a problem. When my family are out sailing and we see something big coming towards us, we get out of the way, but amateurs don't seem to have any fear. Sail does officially have right of way over power ships in open water, but in narrow channels, yachts should keep clear. Anyone can take out a boat – no tests are required – and I think most of the ferry boats hit one eventually. But ferries are very manoeuvrable ships with good brakes and can pull up quickly.

People often ask me if this is a boring job, but more happens in a forty minute crossing than in a four hour watch at sea when you see and do nothing. Here we can walk round the ship and talk to passengers and crew. These ships are lovely to play with. Play with? Handling them, backing into Portsmouth, berthing, though when I first started, the thing that frightened me most was the speed we went alongside the pier, and how close we got to other ships.

Being a captain on these routes is really like an ordinary job. I go home every day, I'm involved with the local church, and three years ago I took up tennis. I can't do these things on a regular basis, but I couldn't do them at all when I was out at sea.

The Garage Man

Some of the best Isle of Wight garages are run by one man who sells you the car, fixes it, pumps in the petrol, and over the door it says 'Fred's Garage'. That's the ideal situation. But we're a big dealer and you won't see the equivalent of Fred when you come in. We have to overcome this by doing little extra things, like providing free cars when customers' vehicles are being repaired, and pagers with a bleep to tell them when they're ready.

Robert le Brecht, 36, was born in Winchester, came to live on the Isle of Wight when he was 7 and went to Bembridge School. At 18, he worked as a fisherman before being appointed Harbour Master at Yarmouth. Ten years ago he became a junior salesman at Premier Ford garage in Newport but discovered he didn't like selling, moved to the service department and is now the Car Service Operation Manager. He is married to Karen, a psychiatric nurse, who runs a home for eleven mentally ill residents in Freshwater Bay, and they have an 8-year-old daughter. Robert also acts in Murder Mystery Week-ends.

The Isle of Wight is a funny place. In the winter there are no traffic jams and we drive around quite contentedly. Then the sun comes out, the roads warm up and the council starts doing repairs. At the same time, holiday-makers arrive, the car population doubles and everyone is on the phone to the local radio station saying the roads are disgraceful. Autumn comes along, visitors go away and everyone thinks it's not so bad after all.

A fixed link with the mainland? If you ask a genuine Islander, he wouldn't want it. But in the same breath he complains about the price of the ferry. I personally *would* like it, but it takes a lot of weighing up. If you think about it for too long, you think of enough reasons against it as well. There's crime on the mainland, and holiday-makers would come across for the day and not stay overnight. It's like you're pulling up the drawbridge. But from the point of view of trying to run a business, it would be so good to be able to collect parts from the mainland, or nip across for a meeting without having to spend £30 and queue for a ferry. And at times you think, wouldn't it be nice to go for a drive on Sunday with the family, or to the theatre? You're rather trapped here because you can't make a spur of the moment plan to get away.

Mrs Garlic Festival

A festival was started eleven years ago to raise money for a community facility and sports field. Then a local farmer (Colin Boswell) went to America and went to a Garlic Festival and thought this would be a good name for ours. When I was first asked to organize it, I knew nothing about it, but I've always been an organizer and it doesn't really matter what you organize. Now, every year I say I'm not doing it again. It is very time-consuming, but people say, 'You're Mrs Garlic Festival – we can't imagine it without you'.

It's a big family entertainment. There must be at least 100 people showing arts and crafts, and giving demonstrations. In the garlic tent, people cook, and sell garlic mushrooms, garlic beer, garlic ice-cream, garlic bread, garlic prawns. Almost every charity on the Island comes and 50 per cent of the sites are let to them at half

Margery Lanfear was born in Manchester and came to the Isle of Wight in 1954. She became a county councillor in 1973, and has been a governor of a local school for twenty-two years. Eight years ago she began organizing the annual two day Garlic Festival. Her first husband died and she is now married to Harold, a former horticultural lecturer. She has two sons.

price. We also have a competition for a garlic queen and vampire king.

The festival can cost £40,000 to put on, but we've made something like £200,000 for community projects since we started. We've funded the building of a dual-purpose primary school hall and subsidize the running costs; we've bought a 5 acre sports field which we had levelled and drained and got grass growing there for the football clubs. We built a pavilion with changing-rooms and showers and we also own some land in Newchurch.

When Michael Palin came to make a television programme about the Island, he said I must be a very formidable person to put on the Garlic Festival, but that I looked as though I was trying to remember where I'd put my knitting! Do I like garlic? I'm not a fanatic, but I'll try any food.

[Mrs Lanfear says she will not be organizing next year's Garlic Festival.]

The Lady of the Chine

Shanklin Chine is the Island's earliest tourist attraction and has been open to the public since 1817. Keats came down in 1819 and said, 'The wondrous Chine is a very great lion. I wish I had as many guineas as there have been spy glasses in it.' It seems he was very happy on the Island and you can still see where he stayed in Shanklin. I think Longfellow was down too and many painters – there are so many pictures of the Chine it seems to have been a tremendous haunt for the artists of the day. I'm still trying to work out if Turner painted it.

The word 'chine' means a deep narrow cut with water leading through to the sea, and comes from the Saxon 'cup in the rising ground'. It has always been part of the Manor of Shanklin, and is a natural beauty spot with its wildness and grandeur and the most lovely flora. It's just over a quarter of a mile long, covers an area of about 3 acres and was a tremendous smugglers' haunt. The Customs and Excise people had a house in the village and used to come down the chine on horseback as a short cut to the beach – everyone was in smuggling, including my ancestors.

Anne Springman, 64, was born in Shanklin Manor, now an hotel, and lived on the Island until she was 18 months old when the family moved to Warwickshire. She worked on Mirror Group newspapers, for a Russian prince, with a public relations company, a publisher, solicitor, chartered surveyor, and for four years on Harold Macmillan's memoirs. In 1979 she returned to the Isle of Wight to take over the running of Shanklin Chine which her family has owned since 1086. It is a deeply wooded fissure in the cliff, with a path winding down to the sea beside a 45 ft waterfall. She is married to Michael.

Today in the Heritage Centre, we've got an exhibition about PLUTO, which stands for Pipe Line Under The Ocean. This was a project during the last war to carry petrol across the Channel to Normandy for the D-Day landings. The pipeline went from the north of England with a spur to Southampton, came across the Solent and the Isle of Wight and one line went down through the chine. They laid 65 miles across the Channel in just under ten hours. An incredible feat. But an escort ship's anchor snarled it, and the cable snapped after it had been running for nearly a fortnight. It could have been repaired, but the Allies were advancing very rapidly and it had achieved its purpose. They hid all the pumping stations in Shanklin Zoo and among the ruins on the Esplanade, and the Germans never discovered what was going on. It was an immense achievement. I've just published a book about it by historian Adrian Searle.

The commandos trained at the chine for the Dieppe raid and a memorial for Forty Royal Marines Commando was unveiled on the fortieth anniversary of D-Day. This resulted in the formation of an association for all those who trained here and we have a remembrance service every year for them.

All we can now do in the chine is make it more beautiful. I'd like to create a greater variety of plants though it has quite a lot of rare ones now like the liverworts and mosses and royal ferns. But it's very difficult to fight nature here, and I think this is why people like it so much. It doesn't matter how many there are in it, there's still this wonderful atmosphere of peace. It has been a much loved place.

The Blackgang Director

My great-great-grandfather, Alexander Dabell, came from Nottingham in the 1820s when he was 10 or 11 and his father started a lace-making factory in Newport. Alexander became a hairdresser and a typical Victorian showman: he used to take a bear on a chain round Newport and Sandown streets selling hair oil. In 1842/3 he concluded a lease, later a purchase, of a couple of hundred yards of coastline which included Blackgang Chine itself.

Blackgang? If my great-great-grandfather was here, he'd say, 'Oh the name is from an old gang of smugglers and they were so nasty they were called the Black Gang'. He was a good storyteller. In fact, 'black' refers to the colour of the clay in the cliffs, and 'gang' is an old word meaning path. Chine is an Anglo-Saxon word meaning cleft or V-shape. There are about seven or eight around the Isle of Wight coast.

In the 1840s, the Island was becoming the place to go for holidays and Alexander decided to cut paths down Blackgang Chine and promote the legends of the place. He charged 6*d.* to go in, opened tearooms at the bottom of the chine, and a museum of local shipwreck artefacts and a shop at the top. He wrapped visitors' purchases in different coloured tissue paper and if they spent more than a shilling, they could go into the chine free.

In 1843 a dead whale was seen floating just off The Needles and Alexander decided to remove the blubber, have the bones bleached and put the skeleton on display. It's still here in the museum.

The main problem with our business today is that we are situated on the south-west tip of the Island on about 40 acres of land that are falling into the sea – about 10 to 12 ft every year. It varies but in 1949 we lost about 140 ft. In 1979, 170 ft. The original chine gorge Alexander saw as a wonderful tourist attraction is no longer here. We are still 400 ft above the sea with sheer cliffs and marvellous views, but the actual land he bought is no more and we've had to buy land backwards and sideways to enable us to continue the business. In the last year alone we've spent something like £1 million just to keep pace with erosion.

We call it a Fantasy Park now and it has themed areas – Nursery, Jungle, Adventure lands and a cowboy town. We also have a fossil shop, where talks are given for schoolchildren, and a sawmill where the story of timber and wood processing through the ages is told. We've also got something called a talking parrot, which just repeats what you've said, and litter bins that say, 'I'm very hungry, can you feed me?' When a child puts a piece of paper in, it goes, 'Belch . . . thank you very much, that was very nice'.

We open from the end of March to the end of October and a lot of people say it's a pity seasonal places aren't

Simon Dabell, 42, worked with John Lewis Partnership, Ladbroke Holidays and at The Dropping Well in Yorkshire before coming to work at the tourist attraction at Blackgang Chine near Ventnor which his family has owned for 150 years. Last year they also took over Robin Hill Country Park in the centre of the Island. He is married to Julie and they have two children. In his spare time he organizes Murder Mystery Week-ends.

open throughout the year. But those who come for short breaks from October to March, do so because they want a quiet place, a roaring log fire, and some nice country walks. They like to travel round the Island, look at the views, do some shopping. If confronted with somewhere they have to pay to go into, I don't think they'd be desperately keen.

At the Manor

The house was never meant to be open to the public. It was bought as a family home, which it still is apart from the fact that we have a tearoom, shop and winery in our garden. But once we close at the end of the day, we just enjoy it and if we want to have a gin and tonic in the drawing-room, we do. I think it has that lived-in feeling which is not something you can go round with an aerosol can in the morning and spray on. It's loved by us all.

We opened the house to the public eighteen years ago. The financial constraints were just beginning to bite and we realized if we didn't have visitors coming through, we wouldn't be able to maintain the house and garden as we wanted to. There were very few attractions on the Isle of Wight in those days. Now I think it's the most densely populated place for tourist attractions of its size in the country.

I started growing grapes here in 1981. Anthony Goddard, who was then running Barton Manor vineyard, inspired me. I said to him, 'What do you think about starting a vineyard?' And he said, 'You're mad, but I'll give you all the help and encouragement you want as long as it's good competition. If you tar the name of Isle of Wight wine, everyone suffers. We might as well help each other.'

We now produce 6,500 bottles in an average year and sell 99 per cent of it direct from the farm gate at £5.65 a bottle. We'd like to sell it cheaper, but the government doesn't help us in any way whatsoever. VAT must be paid, that's 17.5 per cent, and about £1.06 excise duty. In France, the duty paid is a fraction what it is here. Our MEP came round, made sympathetic noises and said he'd be beating the drum loudly for us, but I've heard nothing since.

Janusz Trzebski, 32, lives in Morton Manor, near Brading. His mother came from Poland before the Second World War, his father, Janusz senior, also from Poland, was an RAF pilot. After the war they opened gift shops on the Isle of Wight and later bought Morton Manor, parts of which date back to 1520. Janusz senior, a former local councillor, is 'the boss', his wife, Jadwiga (known as Jane), looks after the shop. Their older daughter, Barbara, is in charge of the tearooms and younger daughter, Yoli, runs her own pottery business. Another daughter, Krystyna, died of cancer seven years ago. With her husband Ray Young, she had helped restore Haseley Manor, and started the pottery there. Janusz junior is married to Charlotte, has a degree in horticulture from Wye College, looks after the vineyard, makes the wine and is, he says, general dogsbody.

We do have a ghost story. A lady medium once came to the house to see if she could detect anything. In the dining-room she sat down by the fire, went into a trance, and wrote reams of stuff before collapsing on the floor. When she came to, she explained a former lady owner of the house was asking for forgiveness because she'd refused to let one of the gardeners marry one of the maids and they had eloped.

Some years later, I was taking people round the house and one chap asked if he could have a word with me. 'The gardener's cottage, where is it?' he asked. I said, 'I'm sorry, we don't have one.' He said he was intrigued to find out because his great-great-grandfather had been a gardener here and the lady of the house was a right old cow and had refused to let him marry one of the maids. The story had been passed down his family and when he'd heard Morton Manor was open to the public, he said he just had to come and have a look.

The Guide

My father used to work for Mr George Barnes at Morton Farm when he had a dairy, and I remember as a child coming up to Morton Manor with the milk. The Cardell family lived here then and they had afternoon milk delivered. I used to come out of school and get the can and bring it up. You can't see children coming home from school and delivering milk now, can you?

I left school when I was 14 and went to help with the teas at Alverstone Mill Tea Gardens. I worked at Nursery Farm, and then went over to the vineyard at Adgestone, picking grapes. I've always done lots of things and I still do. Latterly I worked at the Roman Villa doing the desk and helping with school groups.

After twelve years doing that, I was thinking of retiring, but one day I was talking to Janusz Trzebski and said, 'I'd like to have taken people round the Manor, I know it so well'. So he said, 'Right, we'll bear that in mind'. And when I finished at the Roman Villa, that's what I did. But I don't call it working, I'm just doing it to help them out. I've been here six years now, so I was getting on a bit then.

Irene Munns, in her 80s and a widow, was born on the Island at Morton Farm, and now lives in Adgestone not far away. She works as a voluntary part-time guide at Morton Manor.

Although I do know Morton Manor well, I had to learn all the history and background and I was three months doing it. Janusz gave me a video about the house, but I didn't get on with that. I said to him, 'If you write the history down I can read it from the book' and that was much better. When I took the first lot of people round, I had the book with me in case I slipped up on something. And I said to them, 'You must excuse me because I've only just learnt it'. But after I'd done it about six times, I didn't need the book. I knew it and was away.

When I've told visitors about the history of the house and furniture, I say, 'Perhaps you wouldn't believe it but when the Cardell family lived here and I was a child, I used to deliver the milk, and the servant used to come to the door with a jug and I had to measure it out, with pussy waiting for a little drop in the saucer. That was every afternoon, Sundays and all.' And visitors all look so surprised. 'Well,' they say, 'no wonder you know so much about the house.' And I say, 'Well, it's been part of my life really.'

I don't come here every afternoon now, just when it gets busy. In the mornings I take my dog out, clean my cottage. Most days I go up on the Downs to see the sheep are alright. They belong to a farmer at Whitwell. He's a long way away and I mean, if someone can keep an eye on them, it's a help. When I can't go, a friend goes. We just see there's no dead sheep about.

It was my late husband's great-grandfather, William Munns, a shepherd, who found the Roman Villa. One day, he put a stake into the ground and couldn't get it any further. He saw a gentleman coming up the road and called him over. 'I don't know what's wrong here,' he said, 'I can't get my stake down.' The man said, 'Well, you know what you've found: the remains of a Roman villa.' It was very unexpected, he never knew there was anything there. There's been a controversy over who found it ever since. The man told the shepherd what it was, but it was the shepherd who found it.

I suppose I'm the sort of person who's always done things and if I had to sit in a chair and not do anything, the time would be long. I was a dog trainer for twelve years. I had an Alsation and when they started training classes on the Island, I was one of the first to go. When I had my last Alsation, I worked with an accordionist and we used to play in shows. He played 'There'll always be an England', I put flags out, and the dog would be taught to go and fetch the Union Jack.

I think I've enjoyed everything I've done. I often think of retiring, then find I'm doing something else. I've done some wonderful things in my life.

The Roman History Man

The villa was discovered in about 1880. A shepherd was putting up some sheep wattles in the fields and struck what he thought must have been solid rock. In fact, on clearing it away in order to get his stakes in, he had found the mosaic that's now in Room 2. Before that, a Captain Thorpe who lived in the village and always suspected there was a run of Roman buildings in the vicinity, had marked a tree and asked for permission to excavate. The actual finding of it is down to the shepherd who put the stake in, but as Captain Thorpe had researched the area for a long time beforehand, I think we must give credit to both of them. It was excavated in the main between April 1880 and 1884.

This is probably the only Roman villa in this country that has so many mythological stories in its mosaic floors, and the big floor in Room 12 also has more figures than any other Roman villa in the country. It has become internationally famous, which is why we have to have a new covered building to protect it. The part we can see is AD 240 but after excavations done this year, we suspect the ground was a working farm for a longer period than that; on the field facing the villa, we found first-century evidence of Iron Age pottery, and flaked-off flint. These suggest occupation of the site could go back perhaps 5,000 years. In a survey with a magnetometer which measures the resistance in the soil, there's a suggestion there might even have been hut circles here too.

This villa would have been the home of a very educated Roman, perhaps someone in administration with the Roman occupiers. The estate was probably run by a bailiff on his behalf, and he might only have come during the fine

Neville Carr, 52, was born on the Island and joined the police force as a cadet when he left school at 19. He spent twenty-five years on the mainland with the Hampshire Constabulary before returning to serve his last four years as an Inspector at Shanklin. He retired in 1991 and is now the site manager of the Roman villa at Brading. He is married to Eileen and they have three children.

weather months and brought his family to a very peaceful part of the country. There's no evidence of any battles here.

In the villa's three wings, there would have been a house for the owner, one for the manager – this has a central heating system in it – and one for farm workers or slaves. We know of up to ten Roman villas on the Isle of Wight, but the public can see only two – this one and one at Newport. There's a suggestion that there are two others not yet excavated. I dream of discovering one myself. There is an enthusiasm for this kind of thing now on the Island and a brand new museum is being set up in Newport to house a lot of archaeological evidence not yet on public display.

Until two years ago, the villa was owned by the Oglander family on whose land it is, and they've been on the Island for 900 years. Mrs Oglander still lives on the family estate at Nunwell, and John, her son, works here, but the family couldn't afford to put up a building to protect the floors which were being damaged by bad weather, so they set up the non-profit making Oglander Roman Trust for this purpose, and English Heritage are responsible for the floors. The site has always been open to the public and I have an article written by Conan Doyle who came in 1884 to do some photography. I'm afraid he was very unkind about the guide. 'At a short distance,' he writes, 'this Roman villa looks more like a quarry than anything else. And the tourist has to content himself . . . with a remorseless guide who explained the habits and customs of the "hancient" Romans in a manner that was more amusing than trustworthy.'

One of the most interesting mosaics is the one found first. It has two mythological winged gryphons, a human-style figure with a cock's head and no one can interpret it for us. It could be an Egyptian god or a cartoon on the reigning emperor of the time whose name was Gallus. Or perhaps it was someone taking the mickey out of an emperor who was never likely to come here and see it.

We do have stories about the well here, where a human skeleton was discovered only 12 ft from the top. It appears to have been a 13- or 14-year-old boy and he was found with skeletons of three dogs. There are a lot of theories about how he got down there, but I had a lady come here recently who said she was psychically receptive. She asked me if I knew anything about the people who lived here or the final destruction of the villa. I told her I thought it may well have burnt down. Yes, she said, it had a very violent end. She told me she had the ability to hear what had gone on before in historic buildings. I asked her to go to the well. When she came back she said there was a very faint echo. 'But, I can tell you that this was an accident. It's a 13-year-old boy who fell into the well looking for something – it could have been a pet – and the top of the well collapsed on top of him so no one knew he was there.' This story has only come to light in the last few months.

I think the whole of Roman history here is so fascinating. We were occupied for 400 years. Perhaps some of my ancestors were here – I was born a stone's throw away. You might think this is daft, but I come here in the morning sometimes and I speak to the walls. I say, 'Come on, tell me, what went on here?' But I don't hear anything. And I know a colleague does the same. Perhaps we're all a bit mad here.

The Waxworks Man

When I got fed up with the property business, I decided to have something more permanent. My father owned two little Elizabethan cottages in Brading and I bought them from him to restore. When I started to knock away the plaster I found most of the structures were very early Tudor, but we also uncovered original Anglo-Saxon fire pits, and even Roman remains. I decided not to sell the cottages, and to turn them into a museum of Island history using wax figures. Our first was King Charles. He landed here at Brading (then the chief port of entry) and used to come up past our house on his way to Nunwell House, home of the present Oglander family since 1066. The museum became one of the leading attractions on the Island; there were only three or four others at that time.

There are now forty or so scenes in the museum and some years ago we opened a Chamber of Horrors because I enjoy blood and guts and we know children like it; there's also a world of natural history. All the exhibits are

Graham Osborn-smith was born in Portsmouth. His father was a film producer and as children, Graham and his two brothers and three sisters acted in many films. He served in the Navy during the war, then worked in the property business in Jersey until he came to the Isle of Wight and ran an estate agency here. He also worked in the canning and freezing business and set up an *haute couture* company. Thirty years ago he opened the Wax Museum in Brading, and ran it with his wife and sons until he sold it this autumn (1995). It is now owned by The Needles Pleasure Park but his sons, Stuart and Cameron, will continue to manage it.

connected with the Isle of Wight and I think my favourite is Sophie Dawes. She was a winkle picker in Brading Harbour at the end of the 1700s and then worked at The George in Portsmouth. From there she went to a house of ill-repute in London, where the exiled Prince de Conde saw her and took her back to Paris after the fall of Napoleon. She became fabulously rich and very powerful and almost brought down the French monarchy. She came back to Brading to escape the guillotine and died of dropsy in London. We've reconstructed a room showing her in all her regalia in about 1815.

Another favourite of mine is Valentine Gray – a little chimney-sweep who was beaten to death by his employer who was then hauled up before the court and imprisoned. After that, boy chimney-sweeps were outlawed. Valentine Gray is buried in Church Litten graveyard in Newport and there's an obelisk in his memory.

The museum is open every day of the year, even on Christmas Day and my wife and I have been in on that day for the last thirty years. Two or three years ago, it was quite cold and windy, but when we got to the museum at 10 o'clock, there were six people standing outside, quite annoyed we weren't there! But they were delighted that something was open and that's why we liked doing it so much. It didn't ruin our Christmas Day. It's something I always looked forward to and so did my wife. We took a sandwich along for our Christmas lunch, and a bottle of wine, and I'd put our mince pies on a night storage heater in the main office. We did have Christmas Day off last year – two of the staff volunteered to come in, and our family gave us a lovely lunch. It was the first time we'd had a proper family dinner and I didn't enjoy it at all!

The Town Planner

Although I lived on the Island, I'd never been to see the Model Village until it was up for sale. A fellow called Damms, an engineer, started it in the early '50s and died a few years later. The original models were of Shanklin, built by people at Elstree film studios, and the workmanship is superb. When I came here, I thought: we're in Godshill, we ought to have a model of that. So we started building one. Now the upper garden, the Shanklin end, is pre-war with people dressed in Edwardian/Victorian fashion, and down in the Godshill part, we have the punks.

I consider a genuine model village is a modern day folly in the way that men of money and substance built wonderful towers because they wanted to. It is a folly. Who in their right mind would go and put a lot of small houses in their garden?

I design the models and they're all made on the premises, first in clay, then resin. There are several hundred figures and about forty houses. They're very time-consuming to create, specially the tiny thatched roofs made with bundles of straw; the church alone took 600 hours to make.

Robin Thwaites, 70, was born on the Island. When he came out of the RAF in 1947, he started a small model aircraft shop in Newport before moving to Portsmouth. He returned to the Isle of Wight twenty years later and now runs the Model Village at Godshill. He is married to his third wife, Janice, and has a son, a daughter and a step-daughter.

I'm not a professional, I can't make things to the millimetre. I make them in the style I want, and as long as they look right, I'm not too worried how exactly to scale they are. It's a fun thing. If you want to see professional engineering models, go to the Science Museum. If you want an entertaining half-hour in a nice garden, and have a sense of humour, come here.

A couple of years ago we got an award from the Places of Interest Association on the Island and this was regarded with some consternation in certain quarters because we're not really very big and Godshill is regarded as a rather infra dig place. If local councillors can't think of anything else derogatory to say, they say, 'We don't want another Godshill'. And yet it's probably one of the most up-together places in tourism that you'll come across. There's no candy floss or amusement arcades and most of the attractions are very well kept.

I'm pretty irreverent. I wouldn't join the local council because I know I'd lose my temper and storm out and that would be the end of it. Here I'm chief planning officer, parks superintendent, and anything else I want to be. I'd like to build an airfield next. It will have old-fashioned planes on an old-fashioned landing field where they probably had a lorry with a 50 gallon drum on the back and a hand pump. It may take some people back to that period, and show others what it was like. This is the folly bit.

The Rare Breeds Family

Hugh Noyes, 67, went to school in Canada and the USA during the Second World War, came back to Britain at the end of it, and joined Westminster Press as a journalist on their regional papers. He became *The Times* Parliamentary Correspondent and commuted to the family home in the Isle of Wight at week-ends. In 1990 he was appointed High Sheriff and the same year opened the Rare Breeds Park and Waterfowl Park near Ventnor. He is the son of the poet Alfred Noyes, is married to Judy and they have five children.

My parents bought this place in 1929 and ran it as a dairy farm. But it wasn't until 1982 that I decided to leave London and make the land we owned here more commercially viable. But then the milk quotas were introduced and we were having to throw away the equivalent of 3,000 pints of milk every day. We weren't even allowed to give it away.

Then Judy and I ran into Joe Henson who runs the Cotswold Farm Park, the first rare breeds park open to the public in the country, and we felt it was just the sort of thing we wanted to do. We had a beautiful site and this would enable us to keep animals here, rather than sell off the land for building development or a golf-course.

We're still in the throes of creating it, but it's very satisfying for Judy and myself, and it's brought three of our family back here to work with us. We all have our own speciality: Robert, 26, is on the rare breeds side and supervises the breeding programmes; Penny, 30, looks after the dairy herd; and Clare, the youngest, runs the gift shop. Judy is overall supremo in café and shop.

The Rare Breed Survival Trust has a priority list which consists of animals they consider are becoming close to extinction or endangered. There are between thirty to forty breeds on the list and we try to keep about six or seven animals from each. We have ten different breeds of cattle including the White Park that came over with the Romans, and the Gloucester cattle that helped Sir Edward Jenner produce his smallpox vaccine. We have Beatrix Potter's favourite Herdwick sheep from the Lake District; a lovely little seaweed-eating sheep from the Orkneys; and Portland sheep which are said to have arrived in this country off a galley that sunk off Portland Bill in the Spanish Armada.

We have some Guernsey goats which very nearly became extinct during the war because they were almost all eaten on the island of Guernsey and only saved because one very brave lady hid a few in her cellar. Our Bagot goats are descended from those handed over to Sir John Bagot of Bagot Park in Staffordshire in the time of the Crusaders, and we have over 100 different species of waterfowl, poultry and pheasants.

One of our rarest animals is a splendid cow called an Irish Moiled, a word meaning 'little mound' which is what it has on top of its head instead of horns. There are only about forty left in the world. Our two arrived the size of a pinhead in a block of frozen ice from Liverpool University that has a project going to save the breed by a process known as embryo transfer. The embryos were gradually unfrozen and placed in the wombs of our ordinary Friesian cows. Then over a normal gestation period, the two calves we have now, were born. It was the first time it had been done with this particular breed.

Some of the approved rare breed park owners are absolute purists and will have nothing except animals on the Trust's priority list. We've departed a little from this because on the Isle of Wight you get such a diversity of visitors and they're not all interested in the virtues of rare farm animals. So we have rheas and miniature falabella horses from South America, a few miniature donkeys from Sicily, some wallabies and llamas.

It's fascinating to feel we are able to safeguard rare breeds from dying out.

The Doll Collector

I longed to come back to the Isle of Wight. I couldn't get it out of my blood. So, when we were becoming well-known doll collectors on the mainland, and my husband was ill, we decided to buy a small neglected cottage in Brading High Street and turn it into a doll and toy museum.

The collection started when my daughter, Katherine, was 10 and was given some dolls by relatives going abroad. One day she said how much she'd love to have a Russian doll – that was in 1960 and you know what it was like then with the Russians. But one day she picked up a newspaper and said, 'Look, there's a man mentioned here who's fond of children. Do you think if I wrote to him, he'd send me a doll?' 'What's his name'? I asked. It was Mr Kruschev. My daughter asked me where he lived. I said, 'Oh, just send the letter to "The Kremlin, Moscow", and put "please forward" on it.' Of course, I never thought it would get beyond the London Post Office, but four months later a little nesting

Margaret Munday Whitaker, 72, is a fifth or more generation Islander on her father's (Hicks) side, but was born on the mainland. She served in the WRNS on the Isle of Wight during the war, was married at 18, and has been widowed twice. She lived in the New Forest and Oxford before returning to the Isle of Wight where she started the Lilliput Antique Doll and Toy Museum in Brading. It is now run by her son and daughter-in-law, though she gives lectures on the subject of antique dolls and toys and her life in the WRNS. The museum won a BTA 'Come to Britain' trophy award in 1983.

doll arrived from the Kremlin. She took it to school and as a result of local publicity, it made not just British, but world headlines. We were absolutely overwhelmed with newspaper and TV people. Katherine went on the *Tonight* programme with Cliff Michelmore and Derek Hart and people rang up while she was on air, offering her dolls. For a year or so they were still coming in.

So I got involved myself. I went round visiting museums that had small sections of antique dolls, lecturing and doing charitable exhibitions, and I still do. We've got about 2,000 dolls on view here at Brading, as well as toys. They are all pre-1945 and come from round the world, but mainly from Germany, France and America. We only get them from their original owners or their descendants, so we have stories about each one. The earliest two figures we have – some stone toys – are from a 2000 BC Egyptian tomb which was discovered at the turn of the century by a West Country vicar. The figures had been put in the tomb as servants for the dead person, and I bought them from the great-grandson of the man who found them. I bought some little cotton dolls from their original owner in Devon, that had been given to her in 1905 as a reward for good attendance at school. Another elderly lady asked me if I'd like a wax bride and bridesmaid from 1840 that had belonged to her husband's great-grandmother. If you pull a wire from their chest, their eyes open and close. An even earlier doll was made in Soho in the late 1700s by one of Princess Caroline of Germany's ladies-in-waiting, who had found a remnant of the princess's wedding gown, and dressed a waxed doll in it. She later gave it to a London hospital that raffled it. The winner was Sir William Sorby, a surgeon present at the first public showing of Stephenson's *Rocket*, when a number of people had been injured protesting at its 25 miles an hour speed. The doll is in the museum in a box covered with the newspaper of the time.

We have one doll just 6 in tall, dressed like an animal. It had been given by Queen Victoria to a 3-year-old girl at a Christmas party at Osborne House in 1885. She had kept it until she was 93, and then sent it to me because she said, she'd like to feel it was always going to be looked after.

I've been giving talks about dolls and toys for many years now and it's quite surprising how many schools are interested. I always say to 10- or 11-year-old boys, 'I bet you didn't want to come in'. And they say, 'No, we didn't.' Then I say, 'You wait till we've finished.' And do you know, when we've finished the stories, the boys come up and thank me and say it was marvellous. Somehow I can talk to children and make things interesting. That's what the teachers say, anyway.

The Head Custodian

Osborne House was bought by Queen Victoria in 1845 for about £26,000. It was far enough away to be peaceful, and close enough to the mainland for her to get back quickly. But she soon realized it wasn't quite the house she needed and Prince Albert and Thomas Cubitt redesigned and added to it. It was a very happy place for them and in 1851 they brought a 'Swiss Cottage' over from the mainland, so their nine children could learn about housecraft and cooking. This was Prince Albert's idea – he was very much ahead of his time. The cottage had a kitchen and dining-room and each of the children had their own vegetable plots. These have now been restored to how they were at that time.

Brian Driver, 53, was born in Ryde and worked in UK supermarkets until 1985 when he applied for a 'more satisfying' job at Osborne House. He began working in the shop and became head custodian in 1990. He is married to a police court liaison officer.

When Victoria died in 1901, Edward VII didn't like Osborne House and gave it to the nation. Part of it became a convalescent home for retired officers and this is now run by the Civil Service, with Osborne House itself by English Heritage. Last year we had 175,000 visitors, but in the '70s and early '80s there were about 300,000. We have 25,000 schoolchildren coming between April and June and the house is broadening its appeal to American and Japanese markets. English Heritage promote all their sites as a whole and we can only advise the marketing department in London. I go with my area manager to different trade shows on the mainland but I don't think I'd get any money to go to America to promote Osborne, as I'd like to do.

My favourite room is the sitting-room where you feel Queen Victoria has just gone to church or to attend matters of State. The whole house, within limitations, has been left like this. We've tried to recreate that lived-in atmosphere, as if it was still a family home of which Victoria was very much a part. I visited Buckingham Palace a few years ago, but it didn't have that feeling as Osborne does.

The present Queen came here in 1987 and I think it's been her only visit. When they were preparing for it, they decided the Queen and Duke of Edinburgh should have the use of the two staff toilets. They were duly cleaned and a notice put on the door of one of them: 'Please do not use – for Her Majesty the Queen'. The house supervisor led the Queen towards the toilet, took her handbag, and as they turned the corner, there was the notice still on the door. I think the Queen said, as she went in, 'How quaint'.

The Housemaid

Kathy Barter, 55, was born on the Isle of Wight and has worked at the Osborne House convalescent home for officers and civil servants, for the last forty years. She writes poetry, has written and illustrated two not yet published books, and holds open days in her garden to raise money for a Zambia mission hospital and the Isle of Wight hospice.

I was the fifteenth housemaid living in when I started in 1955. There were six parlour maids, the governor's maid, kitchen maids, valets, nurses, matron and supervisor. Everyone was resident. I was the last one left to live in and they eventually found me a cottage in the grounds.

We, the housemaids, were woken up at 6 o'clock in the morning by the nurses and had to report for duty at 6.30. I had to clean the Night Sister's room before she came to bed, black lead the grates, set the fire, scrub another stone stair, and do a lot of rough work that isn't done at all now of course. I worked as a housemaid until I was 18 and then matron said, as I was of age, would I like to go in the dining-room? I was there for the next eighteen years.

It was a step up and I had to be trained for it. You learnt how to wait at table properly, how to hold the vegetables a certain way – I had roast potatoes all over the table once – and we were told off if we had our apron stripes crooked or our cap wasn't right. We had to stand at the head of the table and watch the patients, and as soon as they needed any assistance we had to see to them. The governor always ate with them. He sat at the top of the table and everyone sat in order, starting from the highest rank right down to the bottom. I started looking after the lowest boys and gradually got to serve the Governor's table.

I used to finish work at 2.30 in the afternoon, then had a break, and if you were on tea shift, you had to be back at 4.15. The evening meal was at 7 p.m. and by the time you'd finished that, it was about 9 o'clock. Friday nights were always later because they had to toast the Queen and have prize-giving for games they'd played in the week. It was 9.45 by the time we'd finished and we'd just fall into bed.

You got used to the hours, but you were tied. We had one-and-a-half days off a week, and a half-day alternate Sundays. I always went to see my parents on my day off. I'd help my mother with cooking and cleaning and gardening. On my half-day I'd go down to my grandfather, and if I was late I got into trouble from my aunt. Most of the girls had to go home and do things for their parents.

The patients in those days were very strict and we were brought up strictly with them. We had to say 'Sir' and 'Madam', which I still do; I think I'm the only one who does. At one time we only had officers but now they have Civil Servants and they're different. We used to get a lot of high ranking and famous people. Lord Denning and his wife came. I remember serving them with their supper in bed. We had Lord Slim, he was a very nice man, and Sir Adrian Boult, the conductor. I think it was Stewart Granger, the film star, who I told off for swearing. He'd sit up in bed for supper, and he was carrying on and moaning about something and I said, 'Don't keep swearing, Sir'. I don't think he took much notice.

About 1976 I decided I didn't want to go on to the organizational side of the Home, so I demoted myself and went back to being a housemaid, until the Benevolent Fund took over and things changed altogether. Before, patients came for a week or two. Now we have residents who stay permanently, getting older and older and not able to join in with things. We did have one romance, Miss Wild and Brigadier Simmonds, but they've gone elsewhere. We used to work like a family, whereas now I don't even know some of the nurses' names upstairs. The staff still get a party at Christmas, but you all bring something – it's not the same as before when we had the officers and nursing staff waiting on us.

I've got less than five years to go before I retire. Officially I have to get out of the cottage here, and I don't know what's going to happen then.

The Hotel Story

Robin Thornton, 58, was born in Warwickshire, but came to the Isle of Wight with his parents in 1944. His mother and her sister had previously been caterers for a hotel in Ventnor and in 1948 his parents opened Old Park Hotel in St Lawrence. Robin and his wife Shirley took over the hotel in 1963.

In 1947 my father decided to go for a walk along the cliffs from Ventnor to the lighthouse. It was the first time since 1939 that it had been safe to do this, because of barbed wire defences put up to prevent invasion. About half-way there, he decided to return home, crossed the field, came to a wall, climbed over it and found himself in a jungle of trees and shrubs. He worked his way through this jungle and came to another huge wall covered in a 4 ft deep cocoon of ivy. Behind it, he found the walls of a building that had been unoccupied since 1906.

It had been a private house and we've traced its history back to 1628. It was owned by the Worsley family until 1806 when the estate was sold, and bought, fourteen years later, by Thomas Haddon, a London barrister who put a wing in each corner of the rectangular building. General Sir John Cheape, a retired soldier from the Bengal Engineers, bought the house in 1858 and lived there until he died in 1875. A subsequent resident, Lord Harrowby, witnessed Queen Victoria making the first-ever telegraph to the Middle East from Osborne House.

In 1881 the British Isles suffered the worst winter in history. Old Park here in the Undercliff had seldom seen snow, but that year there were 45 ft deep drifts. People who'd come for Christmas were unable to leave for six weeks but the household was so self-sufficient, the only thing they ran out of was flour. I have Lady Harrowby's journal describing it all.

After the Harrowbys left, a German industrial chemist, William Spindler, came to Ventnor for his health, and in 1882 bought Old Park with the idea of building a new town. He thought a lot of British health problems were caused by drinking bad water and gave St Lawrence and neighbouring villages their own water supply. He also imported a million trees and shrubs from the Mediterranean and many are still here today. They say that from October to March, Ventnor is warmer than the south of France.

Spindler's son, an artist, was obsessed with Sarah Bernhardt, the actress. Virtually everything he painted was of her and a month ago we found pictures of her acting in plays here in the drawing-room. But, after Mrs Spindler died in 1906, her son and daughter had a row and never spoke to each other again. The house was put into trust and, because neither would release it, it remained empty from 1906 until my father found it in 1947.

This year (1995), for D-Day celebrations, we managed to round up thirty-two WAAF radar operators stationed during the war at RAF St Lawrence. This is just 250 yards down the road from the hotel and none of them had ever seen this house. They couldn't believe it hadn't been built after the war. It had been completely invisible. Amazing isn't it? How do you lose a house?

There is one more story. About two years ago I was working on the hall landing, it was about mid-day. I am a total disbeliever in ghosts, but I saw in my glasses, as you might see in a plate-glass window of a shop, the reflection of a Victorian maid coming out of the door at the top of the hall, walk past me and disappear down the stairs. She had a lace cap, a grey and white striped long dress and a frilly white apron.

When I was doing research on the house, I discovered there had been a maid, Jane Saunders, who one day in 1799 had taken the children down to the beach to see a shipwreck. The cliff had fallen, killing her and one of the children.

A good eighteen months after I first saw the ghost, a mother came to ask if the house was haunted. She'd found her little boy sitting up in bed and calling for her because an 'old-fashioned' lady had just tucked him up. Six months later, another parent came to say they'd seen a Victorian lady in the same room. Last autumn, I was telling a visitor I'd seen a ghost but not the full story, and she went to the bedroom. 'Did you see it?' I asked her when she came down. 'Oh yes,' she said, 'we talked for about quarter of an hour. She told me she can't leave here because she's trapped in the house because of her unexpected death.' So that's three people who've seen her. But I wouldn't have her exorcized, she's much too nice.

The Donkey Ladies

Lorraine Timothy, Carisbrooke Castle: I've been into horses ever since I was a child but I'd never worked with donkeys before coming here. When I saw the advertisement

Lorraine Timothy, 26, has lived on the Island since she was 2 years old. When she left school, she went on a YTS course in a livery yard, and in 1987 started work at Carisbrooke Castle as seasonal custodian. She is now the castle's head donkey keeper, works in the shop, the ticket office, and does the accounts. She is also voluntary welfare officer on the Island for a sanctuary in Devon that cares for 6,000 donkeys.

for a donkey keeper at Carisbrooke Castle, I applied and I've been here ever since. They've had donkeys working the treadmill at the castle well for 300 years and they used to have to walk for a good five minutes at a time to bring up just one full barrel of water. Nowadays it's just an empty barrel used for show. In summer we do a demonstration every fifteen minutes, less frequently in winter.

People come back year after year just to see them. I give a lecture that usually lasts about seven minutes and go through the names of the donkeys which is the bit most people listen to – Josephine, Jennifer, Jessica, Joseph, Jacob, Jubilee and Elizabeth.

Occasionally visitors say we shouldn't work the donkeys, but when they've seen it, they're okay. It's the ones who refuse to come in that go away thinking it's cruel. But I know the donkeys thoroughly enjoy it. How? Their ears are usually forward; and if you give Josephine a day off, the next day you go down to the field where they all are, open the gate, and she'll trample straight over you to try and get out and up to work. She'll put up with one day off, but if you try another, you've had it. Josephine is the eldest, she's 23. Our youngest is Jubilee, who's 18 months old and won't work for a few years yet. We find them all over the place, and they live a long time so we don't need new ones very often. This is their home for life.

I go down in the morning, feed them, muck them out, groom them, clean their feet, bring a couple up to work, and at the end of the day it's the same all over again. Because they are stubborn, people think they're stupid, but it's the opposite. They have minds of their own, and if they don't like something, they will just lock their bodies up and not budge. In fact, I think donkeys are more intelligent than horses. They bond so closely that if one is taken away, the others may die. If something really stressful happens there's a rush of fat into the bloodstream which clogs all the major arteries and they can die quite rapidly. It's called hyperlipaemia.

In April, May and June we have free educational visits and you can get up to thirty school parties a day, averaging fifty children in each. It's a good way for them to learn history. Charles I was imprisoned here before being taken to London to be executed. The castle goes back to 1070, and has been added to ever since. The last person to live here was Princess Beatrice, Queen Victoria's youngest daughter, and she was Governor of the Island. The castle is still the Governor's official residence.

We have re-enactments here, mainly the civil war, and there are chaps dressed up as soldiers parading and doing drills, with lots of shouting and clanging of swords. About fourteen staff do guided tours in costumes. I have a blue Tudor dress with a hoop.

The part of the castle I live in was once the prison block, and I believe it's been used as servants' quarters too. There's a tunnel running from it over to the Great Hall. They did a lot of cooking here at one time and rather than have to go out into the courtyard when it was raining, they took the food through the tunnel. I have been through it – it's very creepy.

I think the villagers here at Carisbrooke do feel this is their castle and help to look after it. Some walk round the moat with their dogs very regularly and if there's any sign of trouble, they'll be on the phone to let us know.

Cherryl Clarke, The Sanctuary: It started with one donkey, Dillon, that we took on as a pet. I had had ponies when I was little but we soon realized donkeys were a bit different and that you mustn't keep them on their own because they hate their own company. So we went out looking for a companion for Dillon and found two that were badly looked after. When people started hanging over our gate and saying, 'Can we come and see your donkeys?', we decided to register as a charity and let in visitors. In 1990 we turned the work into a full-time job.

Cherryl Clarke, 36, was born on the Island. She was employed in local government and her husband Charlie, 53, was a postman. In 1987 they opened a donkey sanctuary at Betty Haunt Lane, near Newport, and in 1994 moved it to a 35 acre site at Lower Winstone Farm, Wroxall. They have three children and work full-time at the sanctuary.

Many donkeys go from home to home because they live so long, sometimes up to fifty years. Children have them but then don't want them when they've grown up, and the donkeys often end up in markets to be sold for pet food. There are also ex-beach, and retired working donkeys. We take in about 20 or 30 a year and have just over 100 here now. The elderly donkeys tend to die in winter months through old age.

We manage purely on donations. Our Adopt-a-Donkey is our main fund-raising scheme. People can choose a donkey from a booklet, and for £15 a year they get a certificate of adoption and a newsletter. We have 7,000 people on the scheme now from about thirty countries. When their adopted donkey dies, we write and ask if they'd like to carry on with another.

We need twenty or thirty people to one donkey to raise enough money to look after them all. It takes about £100,000 a year to run the sanctuary, which is a lot of money to find. The farrier comes every week, the vet is here quite a lot, the food bills are horrendous. We're looking at £1,000 a month. We have a small shop selling animal-type souvenirs, fluffy donkeys, T-shirts with our logo, and I make rosettes for horse and dog shows. I get a huge mail bag every day and the twice-yearly newsletter generates feedback.

What's so special about donkeys? They're so loving towards people and they're not stupid. They have brains. Most people call me the Donkey Lady and think I'm being insulted, but I'm not. They have their own character and they look after each other, too. If you have a sick animal, the others will know. And if one's got to be put down, they all realize something's going on and stand and listen and watch. It's as if they're all waiting to hear news of what's happening.

A donkey's big long ears and loud voice come from its ancestry. They used to live in the mountains of Asia and had to have loud voices and big ears to call and hear each other. When they're on their own and they bray, they're only calling to another donkey in the area.

If I had the money I'd like to build a veterinary hospital here because there's a huge shortage of facilities for bigger animals on the Island when they need X-rays and operations. The Isle of Wight is the most heavily populated county in Britain for horses per square mile – we have about 3,000 in total. But at present, animals have to go to Liphook in Hampshire before they can be treated in hospital.

The Cattle Dealer and Knackerman

We had a small abattoir for the wholesale meat trade at the time I took over, and a knacker's yard for pet food. The abattoir closed in 1960 and the Island's only remaining one shut in 1987, which left us without any facilities here for killing meat for human consumption. We went to local supermarkets and said if we built a new abattoir, or took the existing one over as a farmer co-operative, would they do business with us? They said no. We were charging 80p a pound for beef to butchers, and supermarkets were buying nationally for 76p a pound. They were getting the best beef for less money than we were selling to their local competitors. There was nothing we could do about it.

Every cow or fat animal that's produced here and needs to be sold, now has to go to the mainland. This costs us about £15 for carriage on each animal, and they lose half a cwt by travelling. That's manure coming out. You load them on to a lorry at six in the morning, they keep dunging and the weight comes out of them. A farmer near the market can load his animal half an hour before and go straight there. In fact, he's selling a wheelbarrow of grass with each one.

I now run a refrigerated lorry service for any cattle that aren't fit to travel alive, like a cow with a bad foot, or a bull with a broken leg. European regulations allow us to slaughter them on the farm if a veterinary surgeon is present, but we have a very tight time schedule after that. We have to get the animal to either Farnborough or Seamington near Bath within three hours of it being slaughtered. So it's flag down and non-stop go. We run that service once or twice a week, but it costs about £150 a trip. If there are a lot of casualties, the lorry is away, and the vet says an animal has to be put down, it has to be used as pet food. Money can't come into it, it has to be welfare.

I do a lot of business buying and selling cattle on the mainland. I learnt to bid after the war, buying harness at farm sales when horses were all going out of fashion, and I've still got a lot of them here. I enjoy carriage driving and we have vehicles here that are 120 years old. We still have some that were built for Queen Victoria, and one for Princess Beatrice which was commandeered and used during the war to deliver milk to customers.

I go foxhunting. University students come and call me names and tell me to get off my horse and carry it, and I say well, I feed it seven days a week, it's entitled to carry me for one. They just don't understand. I talked to Rotary

David Biles, 60, the third generation of his family to be cattle dealers and farmers on the Isle of Wight, took over the business when he was 24. He has been Chairman of the Isle of Wight Point-to-Point, Vice-chairman of the Agricultural Show, and National Chairman of the Knackermen's Association. He now farms 400 acres and has a specialist herd of beef cattle. A heart by-pass operation, he says, has enabled him to continue riding, driving horses and lorries, going to market and working a twelve hour day, which includes making after-dinner speeches. His wife Diana runs the clerical side of the business, and they have a son and daughter.

the other night and the first man said, 'Well, we've got to get rid of fox hunting'. And I said, 'Well, when you have, do you realize there's 300 packs of hounds in the country that pick up the majority of fallen stock, mainly calves and sheep which would never be viable for a knackerman to do?' If hunting is stopped, those stock will remain in the fields and rivers, or have to be buried with the possibility of spreading disease to our national water supplies.

I think our business will eventually close and there will be no facilities for sick animals on the Island. There are less than eighty knackermen in the whole country. People are just going out of business because it's no longer viable. We went before a Select Committee and the verdict at the end was that the knacker industry needed an injection of £6 million. The Minister of Agriculture then, said it would find its own level and gave nothing.

We have to be in the phone directory as licensed horse slaughterers, so that if a veterinary surgeon has a pony injured on the road, he knows who to contact, and I get threatening phone calls from the animal rights people. I say that's fine, go and blow my premises up, and you come and deal with animals when they get injured on the road at 2 o'clock in the morning and the police phone. We had a case a few years ago when twenty-one cows got struck by lightning under a tree; seven got up, fourteen died. That was a massive pollution problem we dealt with – the cows were removed within two hours. If I stop trading there will be nobody else to deal with things like that.

It can be quite upsetting dealing with injured animals. Cows are no problem, but a horse is always stressful. You only have a very small space to do your job properly with the bullet. You draw a line from the eye to the ear and use a humane killer, but if it moves you don't do the correct job. And you not only have to deal with the problem of the horse being put down, you have the owners to help as well. A horse does take something out of you when you have to do this.

Student vets at college only have very limited facilities to practise shooting live animals and they sometimes have to use papier mâché heads. But the Knackermen's Association is now assisting with this nationally. If we get students here, I try to arrange for them to have an old horse that has got to be put down, and let them do it under my supervision. Well, papier mâché isn't like the real thing that's moving its head or in pain in a windy lane on a dark night. It's not like that at all.

The Farmer

We were tenants here until 1980 when I took on the farm. It's predominantly dairy, but we grow some cereals to feed to the cows, and rear all our young stock. I also do the insemination of the cows. We've recently reduced the herd to about 130 but I'd like to be up to about 150.

The milk industry altered tremendously after November 1994. Previously everyone sold to the Milk Marketing Board, but now farmers sell to dairies direct and I chose to work with Unigate with a group of local farmers. I have a farm manager, his brother looks after the cows, and another farmer friend comes in to help. We all share the labour really.

When the milk quota system was introduced, ice-cream was not included in the regulations and this gave me the opportunity to expand without buying more land. We now produce ice-cream, clotted cream, cheesecake, luxury desserts, puddings and pies. In the peak season we can make about 180 litres of ice-cream a day. Everything is sold frozen except clotted cream which has a longer life and we're the only producers of it on the Island. We sell from the farm shop here, to restaurants and hotels on the Island, and from a coffee shop we have in Newport called Cranbourne Rest.

Last year (1994) my two youngest daughters, Sally and Debbie, then 9 and 11 years old, showed young calves in the stockmen's classes at the County Agricultural Show. They've always had a couple of calves at home. They lead them out to the 'hutches' in the morning and take them back to the stable at night. Sometimes you get a child screaming her head off when she's being dragged around the place, which only seems to make the calf go a little faster! The girls get shouted at if they let go but they do seem to enjoy it.

In fact, they look after the calves very well, feeding and bedding them each day even when they're at school. They

Jill Cawood, 43, was born in Gravesend, Kent, and her family farmed in Kent and at Niton on the Isle of Wight. She came to the Island in her school holidays to help on the farm and decided from an early age, she was going to live here. She now owns the 320 acre Three Gates Farm at Shalfleet and runs Calbourne Classics. She is married to her second husband, George, and has four daughters.

can choose the ones they want to take to the show, when they (the calves) are born and we just hope they grow to look reasonably respectable. The sad bit is when an animal has to leave us. I've just had to say goodbye to one 15-year-old. She'd given me some nice daughters to continue her line. But her day had come. We also lost a 15-year-old sheep last year, but that's not a bad age for a sheep. We have about twenty-five ewes, and the children look after them and get attached to them too, so we probably don't send away as many as we ought to.

The Countryside Manager

Tony Tutton, 39, was born on the Isle of Wight. He worked in a garden centre and market garden, and for a tree surgery firm in Cirencester before studying arboriculture at college in Guildford, and forestry at Newton Rigg College in the Lake District. He joined the National Trust in 1977 and worked as a tree surgeon/forester in the Wessex region before returning to the Isle of Wight in 1987. He is now the National Trust's Countryside Manager on the Island. He is married to Cathy and they have one son.

When I came back to the Island, I realized it had changed quite a bit. It used to be a rural sort of place and in ten or fifteen years had become much more suburban. People had moved in from outside, the villages were more developed, and the tourist industry had changed quite dramatically. In my childhood this was based on seaside towns: Shanklin, Sandown, Ventnor, Ryde and a bit of the West Wight. People came across on bucket-and-spade holidays. But the ferries have got bigger and more cars are coming now. Industry has infiltrated the whole of the Island rather than just being focused on seaside resorts.

The National Trust owns 3,800 acres, mostly chalk grassland and coastline, but we do have some marvellous broadleaf woodlands. We own Newtown Harbour, a large estuary in the north-west well known for the birds that over-winter there, as well as some areas of coastline on the south-west popular with bathers and famous for fossils and iguanodon footprints. We also have Knowles Farm at St Catherine's Point, which is very rough and rugged, and a ridge of Downland from The Needles right through to the east. Most of the Downs in England are now ploughed up, but this area supports a complete range of insects, and plant species like spring gentian, horseshoe vetch and orchids. We have five wardens, and a harbour master who looks after Newtown Harbour.

Ecology is very important now, but fifteen years ago it wasn't. The Downs were just seen as pieces of agricultural land, but in the early '80s it was realized that untold damage was being done to these important grassland areas. Now we're aiming to restore them and re-introduce grazing to the sites.

We have a particular problem at Ventnor Down where there's a species known as Holm Oak. It was popular in Victorian times. I suspect the trees enhanced the Mediterranean feel of the villas here, liked the climate, and grew like crazy. It's a more aggressive plant species than anything I've ever seen. The wardens have spent a lot of time trying to get rid of it and about four years ago we introduced a herd of wild goats which are showing signs of being very effective in controlling it. A lot of our work is labour intensive, so if we can get animals to do it instead, that's the way to go.

Some of National Trust land is farmland, but most of it is free of charge for anyone to wander over. People take that for granted and if you cut a piece of scrub or some trees down for woodland management, they misunderstand our intentions. There are a lot of dog walkers on the Island who dislike having animals grazing the Downs despite the fact that this has been going on for hundreds of years. They think National Trust land is public open space, and we have no right to put animals there. They also see it as commercial exploitation rather than being for the benefit of the countryside as it is. We have quite a big educational role to put across why we do things.

The Growers

Colin Boswell, the Garlic Grower: We started growing garlic after I came back to the Island. My mother had put some in her garden in 1976 and it had grown quite well. Our first commercial crop was in 1979. We now have about 30 acres and also import garlic from dedicated growers committed to us in Chile, Hungary, Spain and California.

We supply food manufacturers all over the UK with fresh peeled or puréed garlic for their garlic bread, chicken Kiev, that sort of thing, and much of the fresh garlic you see in mainland supermarkets also comes from us. We sell garlic seed to amateur gardeners, who buy it through catalogues and get good crops because it's acclimatized to the UK

Colin Boswell, 43, came from Kent to the Isle of Wight at the age of 6 when his father started farming here. He worked in market research and advertising on the mainland until returning to the Island in 1976 to go into partnership with his father who was growing sweetcorn. He has been Chairman of the Island Farmers' Union and is on the Isle of Wight Training and Enterprise Council. He is managing partner of Mersley Farms, married to Jenny and they have five children.

climate, and we also produce smoked garlic, smoked garlic butter and puréed ginger. In August every year there's a Garlic Festival on the Island, which was our idea (see page 34).

We employ about 250 staff in the summer months, mostly cleaning garlic and packing sweetcorn. They stay with us a long time and there is a happy constructive atmosphere here. I think they feel they're part of something that's different because there are no other commercial garlic farms like this in England. In the last three or four years we've grown quite fast, which has its own problems, but people like to be part of something that's expanding.

We're also slightly pioneering – there's an atmosphere of innovation here, of trying new techniques. One of the things I'm very proud of at the moment is our new £500,000 packhouse at Langbridge where all the machinery has been built in the farm workshops to a very high specification. We've taken on people from Westland Aerospace to do this, and they've produced something you're unlikely to find in other packhouses. We have a close working relationship with several French growers and supply Marks & Spencer on the Continent. Why are we the only commercial garlic grower in the UK? It is a relatively expensive product and requires an enormous amount of hand labour. Unless you're set up to do it, and have a market for it, it would be difficult to justify.

Our latest venture is to explore the market for fresh herbs in Columbia. A lot of people smile when I tell them this and say, 'Ah yes, I bet you are'. But there are a lot of similarities in the market for herbs and garlic, and we're working with a Columbian company. Every Sunday, a plane comes into Heathrow with tarragon, marjoram, oregano, and lemon grass on board for us.

I think Isle of Wight growers and farmers keep their light under a bushel. We have the best tomato industry in Europe, our milling wheat leaves the Island by boat for countries all round Europe, and 60 per cent of baking potatoes consumed in July in the UK come from the Isle of Wight. A number of factors, including high light-intensity, can give us up to three weeks' advantage even over somewhere as close to hand as Chichester. I say to everybody, if you want a demonstration of the Isle of Wight climate, buy some tomatoes, sweetcorn and garlic, that's demonstration enough.

The difference between imported garlic and ours? If I gave you garlic bread made with our garlic and some made with imported purée, you'd spit the imported one out because it would make your mouth go dry. The trouble is when you eat this in a restaurant, you think it's the garlic doing that to your tongue, so you drink more which is good for the restaurant but not so good for you.

More and more Brits are eating garlic now and I'm very happy this is only just beginning to change. We have a tremendously wide market to go for.

Bob Buckett, the Apple Grower: I planted my first apple trees in the winter of 1936/7. My mother's people were farmers so I suppose I got my love of the land from them. Now I've got half a dozen bush trees and about fifty each of cordons and dwarf pyramids. I also grow pears, plums, raspberries, gooseberries, currants, tayberries, and grapes in the greenhouse. I like growing flowers too, and at one time had 300 roses.

The English apple has almost disappeared really and I think it's quite wrong to have let so many varieties die out. It's basically because not many give such regular heavy crops as Golden Delicious does, but frankly I wouldn't give that house room. I don't think there's really anything to beat a Cox when it's just at the right stage, but Ribston Pippin is good and another nice variety is Ashmead's Kernel. I could hawk my apples round the local shops, but it's not really a commercial proposition. I give them away to families and friends and put the rest at the end of my drive and let people take what they want. I must have given away hundreds of pounds over the years.

I've been exhibiting at our local shows and one or two others for thirty years now. I put up however many varieties I have available. This year I'll probably have seventy-two. I've had my fair share of prizes. I can't tell you how many, but my name has been on the local Chale cup for fruit for eighteen years.

I think I've got the biggest private collection of varieties on the Isle of Wight, but there is one nurseryman at Godshill who may have more. People are quite surprised when they

Bob Buckett, 85, was born on the Isle of Wight and his family have lived on the Island for over 400 years. On leaving school, he went into the family building business started by his grandfather in 1881, and ran it with his brother until he retired nearly twenty years ago. He has been Chairman of Brighstone Parish Council, and is now Vice-president of his local lifeboat branch. He is President of Brighstone and District Horticultural Society, and a Trustee and Secretary of Newport Grammar School charity. In 1962 he was awarded a Silver Gilt Medal by the Worshipful Company of Fruiterers for his twelve varieties of dessert apples. Today he grows over 100 varieties of apples in his half-acre garden at Brighstone and is a judge at local shows. He has had articles written about him in *Amateur Gardening* and *Garden Magazine*, and in 1994 appeared on television's Channel 4 *Gardening Club*. He is married to Margery and has three children, six grandchildren, and three great-grandchildren.

hear the number I have – they don't know there are so many varieties. But anyone who knows anything about them would agree that there's no country in the world that can grow apples like we can. It's the climate, perhaps. There is one variety that's indigenous to the Isle of Wight – its very small and a brilliant yellow – but I haven't got it now.

No, I haven't had an apple named after me. It takes about ten years to prove one worth having. I'm just happy doing what I'm doing.

Jan Wyers, 41, comes from Kent and has lived on the Isle of Wight for fourteen years. She worked in a children's home and started a small herb business before setting up 'A La Carte Daylilies', a mail order company. She now has the only national collection of miniature daylilies (hemerocallis) in the country. She is Librarian of the British Hosta and Hemerocallis Society, is married to Andy and they have one daughter.

Jan Wyers, the Daylily Grower: I'd always been interested in plants and had worked in various nurseries. But when I first saw a daylily in a friend's garden I was totally smitten. I think I've now got in excess of 600 different ones.

I was motivated to start the mail order business because I liked the plant but importing it, mainly from America, became expensive and my addiction got to the point where it needed financial support. I now have about 150 customers on my mailing list from this country and overseas. I've also taught myself to breed the plants and become interested in genetics.

Until I started making a bit of fuss about daylilies they hadn't really been recognized in this country, apart from a few of the older ones, but there are something in excess of 30,000 different cultivars (varieties). The flower was shown at the Royal Horticultural Society in 1941 and in the early 1970s, but as far as I know, no one else has shown them since, and people were really surprised when I took them to the Hampton Court Flower Show in 1995, because they expected muddy oranges and yellows, an occasional red perhaps, but nothing like the range of colours we had.

People think they are very tender plants, but they're as tough as old boots. They first start flowering in late May, they're out in June, fantastic in July, still going in August and September and, if no hard frost, keep plodding on through October. The clumps can be divided every three to five years. They look stunning in large borders and I can't understand why they're not as well known as roses or campanulas. Their history goes back over a thousand years and Confucius wrote about them.

I think there's a lot of prejudice about anything from America and people will grow varieties like 'Pink Damask'

nkle Street in Calbourne, with its
naculately thatched cottages,
lens full of flowers and a stream
ere watercress grows.

A quiet street in Seaview, a village
which instils loyalty among its
holiday-makers. The same families
come over year after year, and many
have bought houses here.

eeting of the ways at Shorwell, a
ge with three manor houses,
ched cottages, the ancient church
t Peter's and a pub.

The entrance to Carisbrooke Castle, where Charles I was imprisoned in 1649.

St Catherine's Lighthouse at Niton, 5 miles from Ventnor, was built in 1840.

Osborne House was the family home of Queen Victoria and Prince Albert from 1846 until the Queen's death in 1901. (*Photo by kind permission of English Heritage*)

Poets and writers have found inspiration in Shanklin Chine, a deep narrow ravine where r plants grow in unspoilt woods and spectacular waterfalls drop down towards the sea.

The beauty of the landscape at Brook Down. (*Photo by kind permission of The National Trust*)

cratchell's Bay, The Needles Headland.
hoto by kind permission of The National
ust)

bats at Seaview.

Deckchairs blow in the wind on the promenade at Sandown overlooking the resort's long sandy beach.

A street in the old town of Yarmouth, near the harbour where the car and passenger ferry boats cross to Lymington.

The Shipwreck Centre and Maritime Museum at Bembridge – six galleries of nautical heritage with Spanish pieces of eight, antique diving equipment, ships' models, and artefacts from local shipwrecks.

A narrow street in Cowes leading down to the sea

and 'Stafford' and not try anything new. It's not just the colours, but the shapes and sizes of daylilies are different, and this meets with prejudice from the higher echelons of the horticultural world. But I don't take too much notice of that because ordinary people like the flowers and they're good garden plants. Hemerocallis, the botanical name for daylilies, comes from two Greek words meaning 'beauty for a day'. But although each flower only lasts a day, they bloom in succession and last year 'Ice Castles' flowered fifty-two days without a break.

We've also got involved in a conservation project for children which I hope will be taken up nationally. The idea is for adults to go into schools and talk to teachers and children about the conservation of garden plants. There's a lot done with wild flowers, but very little with garden plants and if we don't conserve *them*, we'll end up with garden centres just having the more common flowers and a lot of boring gardens. It's the specialist nurseries that need to be encouraged and people shouldn't throw away old clumps of plants before checking they aren't the last of that particular kind.

The Drinkmakers

Anthony Goddard: In life you do lots of things without having done any market research, like saying 'Will you marry me?' It's the same with starting an English vineyard. One has this vision of a patrician existence lying in the sun, picking ripe grapes off vines. But it doesn't turn out like that in real life. It's usually raining or you have galloping mildew.

The best year for growing vines, 1976, was also the worst for planting; the earth was so dry. We planted 3,764 precisely on about 4.5 acres. Now there are 14 acres. Once we started getting visitors in, the vineyard began to pay for itself and our problem was making enough wine, rather than shifting it. We used to say our wine was available at Buckingham Palace, Harrods, the Ritz and on the Isle of Wight, as it was, and we won the English Wine of the Year competition, and several gold and silver medals. Now 95 per cent of Barton Manor

Anthony Goddard, 50, studied farming at Agricultural College, Cirencester, and is a Fellow of the Chartered Association of Certified Accountants. In 1964 he joined the family engineering company, and in 1976 bought Barton Manor, once Edward VII's Isle of Wight home. He planted a vineyard and produced prize-winning wines before the Lloyd's crash forced him to sell the property. He was Chairman of the English Vineyards Association (1987–90), on the English Quality Wine Committee (1990–3), and continues to make wine for the present owner of Barton Manor, Robert Stigwood, the impresario. In 1993 his family acquired Tavern Supplies (IoW) Ltd, and he started Goddard's Brewery, making real ale in an eighteenth-century barn at his home near Ryde. He is a Trustee of the Isle of Wight Charitable Trust, has been married to Alix for twenty-four years and they have two daughters.

wine is sold on the Island and the problem has been producing enough.

The Almighty has a very big input into whether you're going to get a good crop, but making the wine, which is the part I've always enjoyed most, is more scientifically based. There is art in it, too, though not as much as there was. We have a laboratory at Barton, so can do reasonably accurate scientific measurements and on a good year we produce about 25,000 bottles, sparkling, rosé and white wines. You can make jolly nice white wines in England; they're fresh, flowery, aromatic, wonderful aperitifs and Champagne substitutes. I think it was a pity the early pioneers of English wine growing didn't start making sparkling wine, because you actually need high acid grapes for this, and the Champagne district in northern France has a very similar climate to ours. It would have made a lot of sense to have concentrated on producing a high-value premium product like a sparkling wine and built up a cache for it.

When we sold Barton Manor, we thought we'd have enough money to retire gracefully. But I get bored quite quickly, and decided to start a brewery as well as continuing with the winemaking. The great thing about a brewery is that, once you've got the plant in and bought the raw materials, you can start brewing straight away and have something to sell three weeks later.

I have a very good brewer, Jonathan Stancill, and the sort of stuff we're making is traditional real ale using the best raw materials we can get hold of. We used to buy English hops, but the best ones now, I'm ashamed to say, come from North America. We produce a beer called Fuggle-Dee-Dum, a Goddard's Special Bitter, which is a blend of various hop varieties, and Winter Warmer, which is darker and much stronger, 5.2 per cent alcohol. Fuggle-Dee-Dum was voted champion beer of Sussex recently, and a runner-up for the champion beer of Britain. We produced a quarter of a million pints last year.

Jonathan Stancill: My father was a brewer and making beer was the only thing I was ever good at. I had three jobs in breweries where I was paid nothing but I was learning the trade. I did my own training scheme rather than a government-based one. When I was working at Burt's

Jonathan Stancill, 32, comes from Sheffield, and worked in breweries in different parts of the UK before coming to the Isle of Wight. He makes beer for Goddard's Brewery, is the company's only brewery employee, and lives with his partner Bethan and their three children.

Brewery here on the Island, I met Anthony Goddard and he suggested we started a brewery together. He's converted a barn at his home into a fifteen barrel brewery.

I make the recipes up, decide what to do, put it altogether and hope I come out with a decent beer. Being a small brewery we must produce a drink everyone will like, so my job is to get something interesting enough for people to love, but commercially good enough to be able to sell on the open market. I try to make it as near big brewery style as possible, clean, nice beer with a good nose and condition, that's important. But you don't want to make it bland which is what happens when accountants get hold of it. You can drink that kind all night, but you don't actually say, 'Wow, that's *wonderful*'. That's the thing I want to keep.

I think people like to feel when they come to the Island that they are getting something they can't get elsewhere, so I don't want to saturate the mainland market, but try to make the Isle of Wight beer special. I make 2,500 litres every time I brew, and I brew maybe once a week, or every two weeks in winter. I could probably go up to forty-five barrels a week but if we go over that, we'd have to get new vessels, and maybe a helper, because it would knacker me.

We started brewing in the summer of '92 and this is the best brewery I've ever had. I'd say we probably have about thirty outlets on the Island, but only six or seven real Goddard's publicans sell loads of beer very quickly. That's the important thing. Not how many pubs you've got, but how much they sell. My criteria is that you tap the beer, sell it in a night, it will be good, and you'll have another cask waiting to be tapped.

I'm not a brain surgeon. I'm not an airline pilot. All these things require a huge amount of information that has to be sorted out. Making beer is quite simple. I like the simple life though I'd probably like to sell three times as much as we do and have ten people working for me because it does get quite lonely. But I do love making beer.

The Ice-cream Maker

I was in the army for five years and loved it. It gave me the opportunity to continue the education I never had. I studied accountancy and management and when the war was over I

Edward Minghella was born in Scotland of Italian parents who emigrated to Paris when he was 18 months old. After his father's death a few years later, the family moved to Italy. Nineteen years old at the beginning of the Second World War and a British citizen, Edward came to Britain in 1940 and entered the Royal Army Medical Corps with more knowledge of French, Italian and Spanish than English. He came to the Isle of Wight in 1950, and was a local councillor for many years. He now runs the Minghella Ice-Cream Co., is married to Gloria (see page 94) and they have five children and eight grandchildren.

went to work in an ice-cream factory in Portsmouth. They used to make just plain vanilla and I thought there was so much more they could do. When I got married, we opened a café in Ryde and made ice-cream at the back of it until deciding to concentrate on becoming ice-cream producers. We now make some sixty-three flavours – almond, honey and brandy, peach brandy, strawberry and champagne, raspberry and champagne, fudge and almonds, rum and raisins, kirsch and black cherries – I could go on and on.

There can be up to twenty ingredients in one product and they come from all over the world: vanilla from Madagascar, cherries from Italy, ginger from Australia, maple from Canada. We sell our ice-cream all over Britain, do business with Safeway and Tesco and export to France. In fact, we print our package in two languages now. Ice-cream has become a trendy business, a fashionable product, and you have to make new ones every year, like a car company. We employ just under ten people with additional staff in the summer. I taste every batch of ice-cream that's made.

But I'm not a very good businessman. I let my heart rule my decisions more than my head. I work more for the love of it, for the sheer challenge, and also for people. I love to make employees feel part of the business. I believe everyone should contribute to the society they live in either by helping towards education, which is my passion, or by providing job opportunities and training.

I would like to see more quality industry on the Isle of Wight. It's what gives an area prosperity and recognition. When I was on the council, I wanted to create a science park here specializing in energy, its development and application, the saving of wind, sun and sea power. We have all these in abundance on the Island. I never got any support for the idea, but it could have made the Island a place that would have attracted brains and we do need quality skills here. At present quality jobs are not easily available and anyone with ability goes to the mainland. Young people who are ambitious won't stay. Our five children all live in London. Gioia is deputy head of a London comprehensive school, Anthony is a film director and writer, Edana, a senior researcher for the Sainsbury Foundation, Loretta, a lawyer, and Dominic works for TV. I think ice-cream must be good for the brain!

Retire? It's not on my agenda.

The Chef Patron

My mother died when I was ten and I was looked after by housekeepers and learnt to cook by necessity. It was at the end of the war, and food was not readily available, so we had to make the best we could out of very little, which was a great training for a cook.

When I found Essex Cottage it was in a good position, but lacking in character. It was a very old building going back several hundred years and originally two one-room thatched farm cottages belonging to the Worsley family at Wroxall. They sold them in 1852 to the local vicar who I think was from Essex, and that's how it got its name. In those days if you had any standing in life, you certainly didn't own a property with straw on the roof, so the first thing the vicar did was put a new roof on. It was opened as a tearoom in 1853 or 1854. Queen Victoria apparently visited it twice, and her daughter, Princess Beatrice, used to entertain her daughter and son-in-law, King Alphonso of Spain, to tea here.

I always say catering is like a game of cricket. You've got to play to the wicket, not against it. So it's no good putting on high-class food during the day – holiday visitors like toasted tea-cakes, strawberry cream teas and unusual snack-type lunches. In the evening we have traditional English dishes as well as others that I learnt when I was cooking overseas. One of my jobs was working for Picasso for the last eighteen months of his life. I was in the south of France when I saw an advertisement for a chef and it happened to be from him. I learnt afterwards that I, an ignorant foreigner, had stepped in and answered it where locals had feared to tread. They used to revere him, but I was never keen on art myself and let that be known. As a result I got on extremely well with him. Later, I cooked for his publisher in Switzerland and for the Saudi and Moroccan royal families.

Here at Essex Cottage, we try and create a family atmosphere particularly at Sunday lunch time. People come for this from all over the Isle of Wight with children and grandparents, sometimes three or four generations. In France a traditional Sunday lunch is very much a family event, and I try and create that kind of atmosphere here.

Roy Dalby, 62, comes from Blackpool. He trained in the hotel trade, was an RAF pilot during his National Service, worked in the regional crime squad until he had to leave after a serious injury. He was a chef in the Lake District and the south of France, where he became the first English *sous-chef* in a Michelin 3* restaurant. In 1987 he bought Essex Cottage in Godshill, then a tearoom, and opened it as a restaurant a year later. He is now its chef patron. He has been married and divorced and has two sons.

The Fish People

Jo and Salty (Peter) Green are both Island born. Jo, 48, was a social worker for twelve years, Salty, 49, is a fisherman. In 1993 they opened a fish shop in Yarmouth, and two years later 'Saltys' restaurant above it. The business is very much a family affair: their daughter Nicky, 30, runs the shop and helps in the restaurant; their son Jamie, 27, fishes for lobster and crab. They have four grandchildren.

Jo: We go to France quite a lot and I used to see such good fish shops there, and so few here. At that time my husband was fishing in partnership with Jamie, but decided it was getting a bit too much for him – fishing is very strenuous. I thought right, we'll open a fish shop like they have in France. We have the local fishermen here, and our own crab and lobster, and two years ago, we did. This Easter (1995) we opened a restaurant above it, and it's been a phenomenal success.

We have local skate, plaice, lovely seabass that comes in every single day, lemon sole, turbot, trout, salmon, even tropical fish sometimes. The family oversee the lot. If one can't be here, another runs in and takes over: my husband, daughter-in-law, son, there's always one of them around. I do the bar work, greet people, wash up, cook sometimes, work in the shop, a bit of everything. The head waiter Shane helped build the place. Everyone swaps around. We've taught them to be adaptable; today you're in the shop, tomorrow out fishing.

Salty: Of all the shell fish caught in this country 90 per cent of it goes to Spain and France. The English in general are not educated to eat it which is a shame, and you can get more money sending it over to Spain. In the restaurant here, we provide plain, simple fish, don't mess with it. Serve it as it is. Earlier this year, people came here to eat before going to the Yacht Club Ball – they just took the whole place over in their ball gowns.

Jamie fishes up to mid-Channel, about 30-odd miles, but you can go 6 miles off the French coast if you want to. We've had no problems at all with French fishermen. We're not in the huge boats they are and it wouldn't pay the Spanish to fish in the Channel though they probably wouldn't get a licence anyway.

Jo: I think people are struggling to find good places to eat on the Island. A lot of small restaurants went down the pan when pubs went into food in a big way about two or three years ago. The problem for restaurant owners here is that they aren't willing to close down in the winter, and re-open happy and smiling next season. They try and stay open through the winter and can't do it. But from the beginning of October, I'll open only from Thursday to Sunday. After Christmas we'll close for two months completely and re-open for Easter. You have to be a bit ruthless. People say you shouldn't close, it's not fair on the locals. But I think they may appreciate us more when we re-open!

A very controversial issue here at the moment is the development of Yarmouth Harbour. It's run by the Harbour Commissioners who've decided to build themselves a new set of offices. They have a lovely building here, but they want a new one with more facilities, and are spending nearly £1 million to put up a horrendous two-storey block on the other side of the harbour. Plans went through very quietly and no one knew much about it until they started building.

The fishermen's complaint is that this large sum of money is being spent on an unnecessary building, while nothing is being done for them. They don't have a washing-down area or even their own parking space. They get a ticket if they park their pick-up vans by the quay. When visitors come to the Island, they love to watch fishermen unload their catch. At the moment, the men have to come to the side of the quay and quickly chuck off their stuff. If they stay, they're fined.

Jamie: The new building is something out of the twentieth century, in an eighteenth-century harbour. We all accept there need to be facilities for incoming boats, yachts and fishermen, but we don't see the need for a concrete two-storey building so that the harbour master can have a massive board room. It's just ridiculous.

The Editor

Peter Hurst, 56, was born in Southall, Middlesex, and went into journalism from school. He worked on Westminster Press regional newspapers before becoming editor of the *East Grinstead Observer* and later the *Surrey Herald* series. He became editor of the *Isle of Wight County Press* in 1987. He is Chairman of a fund-raising appeal to raise money for an MRI scanner for the local hospital, and sits on a Challenge and Adventure committee, a project for young would-be offenders. He is married to Gloria and they have three children.

The *Isle of Wight County Press* was founded in 1884 by George Brannon and his family, and it's still independently owned. The last Brannon of direct descent is the wife of our present chairman, Mr Richard Bradbeer. Today, the circulation of the paper is 36,608.

On the editorial side, we have about twenty staff and ten village correspondents who are paid around £35 a week. This was something I introduced when I came because I found the paper was very old-fashioned in many respects. Probably someone seeing it for the first time today would say we were still old-fashioned and it's intentionally so. I would describe it as middle of the road, not too abrasive and we try to appeal to everyone.

Local politics are very important on the Island and although we don't take any political stance, we're still accused of doing so by two political parties. But providing we go on being accused by all sides, that's fair enough.

The main difference between an island and mainland paper is that we have more defined boundaries. We only cover the Island and are not interested in anything that happens beyond 5 miles out at sea. We'd like to be able to do investigative-type features, but our problem is there's so much local news and everybody expects every event to be in the *County Press*. People complain about the size of the paper – it has three sections – but I think they quite like it really. We have an enormous number of letters and a freelance chap who researched local papers all over the country, found the number we receive was by far the most. We publish two and a half pages of them and that's probably only 60 per cent of what we get.

There are, of course, the perennial issues. One is the fixed-link with the mainland. That always rouses a lot of correspondence. We did a survey on this, and found two to one were against the scheme. I feel personally it could be a great shame to have one, but I don't think any of us know enough about it.

The main issues at present are the economy of the Island, what's happening in health care, and community care which has been an issue ever since it was introduced two years ago. There is some resentment about the big stores that have opened here – Safeways, Tesco, latterly Marks & Spencer and British Home Stores – and the effects these have on some shops. But other sections of the community have been crying out for them. People were demanding M & S should come here for years before it actually arrived.

There are a majority on the Island who don't like change and that doesn't only constitute Islanders. A very large percentage of people come here because they're looking, either in retirement or younger people too, for a lifestyle that has disappeared from many places on the mainland.

I think we have a problem in that in some ways we're an island, in others we're not. For instance, while the Island Games – held every two years in islands round the world – were successful here, I don't think they quite captured the public imagination they seem to have done in say, Jersey. It's possibly because that's a long way off-shore, dependent on it's own culture. Here, football-wise, people go over to watch Portsmouth and Southampton.

They say editors have to have a tough skin. I don't think I've got one. I'm one of the world's worst worriers. But if you're not a bit nervous about things, it probably means you don't care. You have to have a few butterflies, sometimes.

The Publisher

There are about 150 books about the Island in print now and twenty or thirty new titles published every year, not all by me. There are nine or ten real book shops here, and about forty-five newsagents. I publish about twelve to fifteen titles a year and our authors work on a percentage of net receipts. They don't get very much, but I tell them they're going to get a lot of help and

Neil Hammerton ran away to sea at 15 and joined the Merchant Navy with the Blue Star Line. He did national service with the RAF and has subsequently worked for computer and technical book companies, EMI, Warner Brothers, Music Sales Ltd, starting the Original Record and Tape company in 1977. He met his wife, Jean, when they were both working at Foyles in London. He now runs Hammerton Book Services, publishing books mainly about the Isle of Wight, and distributing others for eight mainland publishers.

encouragement. They can walk in here any time or phone me up. There's a lady in Shanklin who telephones me because her husband hates her writing. She rings up and says, 'Please tell me I'm doing the right thing'. And I say, 'You're doing the right thing, don't worry about it.' Or they ask me to look at a manuscript. A magistrate gave me one of his memoirs recently. He came back a few days later and asked me what I thought. I said, 'Well, I can't publish it.' He asked why. 'You call it "Wide Justice"', I said. 'It should be called "Confessions of an Island Magistrate". You've changed all the names, dates and places and play down every single thing you've done. We must have all the facts. I want to know all about this little room at the back of the court where you have to watch pornographic films.' 'Well,' he said, 'I don't know whether I can do that' and took away his manuscript.

People like books about the Island, warts and all. And I think deep down in every Islander is the thought that if we were a little further from the mainland, we could declare independence tomorrow, to hell with the rest. But because we're only ten minutes across the water, it's an uneasy compromise. You know quite well that, although there's a fire brigade here, if there's a big conflagration, you're dependent on the Hampshire fire service.

The Islanders are tremendous readers and they do deserve a better library service. I went into a library the other day and asked about a current bestseller. The waiting list was nine weeks. The argument is that there isn't enough money to fund it, but you could apply that to most aspects of Island life. It's not a self-sustaining economy.

There are people who would like to see an Island-owned superstore. At present all the money from the big stores is drained back to the mainland, they're sucking it out of the Island economy. Go into Safeways and say you want some Isle of Wight potatoes. They'll say sorry, but they haven't got any. They get theirs from Jersey because they're cheaper. But there has been a bit of improvement this year. We now have an Origin Approved Group which is designed to market products produced here and this is beginning to worry people who bring in tin trays from Thailand to sell, as it should.

The Poet

I knew this was the place where Tennyson and Keats had lived, and at my first interview for the job to run the library in Freshwater, I asked if any famous modern writers lived here. I was told 'not really, but there's a man who dresses in black called David Gascoyne'. I'd been writing about him for my Ph.D and think he's England's greatest living poet so the first thing I did when I got here was to contact him and, with his wife Judy, we set up the Isle of Wight Poetry Society. Through that we've brought some of the best poets in the country to the Island.

The Tennyson Society meets every month, usually in Tennyson's study at Farringford (the house where he lived, which is now a hotel). I think you can still feel his presence, specially behind the house where The Wilderness is; more in the winter perhaps, when tourists have gone, and it's misty up on Tennyson Down.

There are dozens of writers living on the Island – we had a poetry competition once and had over a hundred entries. A lot of them are like me, they've come over almost in retreat from the modern world. Auden and Isherwood lived in Freshwater, D.H. Lawrence wrote one of his first novels here, George Bernard Shaw and T.S. Eliot both came for their honeymoons. It's a place where you can hide from the world. But there's another side to the Island. There's a lot of witchcraft and dark spirits around. It's not just a sunny holiday island. But it is a nice mix of people rooted in the community and landscape.

The trouble is I am very much seen as a renegade by some people in power, who think I'm rather threatening because I don't toe the modern party line on poetry or the arts. I do have standards, but I'm immune to fashion. My poetry is very influenced by landscape, and I tend to write in formal structures. But it's also aggressive, angry poetry about the sixties, and what's happened since. I think society and civilization have declined and become much more greedy and rapacious, and I've been much criticized for saying so. But it's like Wordsworth after the French revolution – you feel a glory has gone and gone needlessly, and the only response is anger and you have to write about it.

Brian Hinton, 44, read English at Oxford, did an MA and Ph.D, trained to be a librarian at the Bodleian Library and decided to come and live on the Isle of Wight 'because the happiest time of my life had been the week-end of the Island's 1970 pop festival'. He came in 1978 to run the library at Freshwater, but two years ago took enforced retirement. He has written a book on the pop festival, and a recent new version of it is sold alongside the official festival video. With Councillor Ron Smith, he ran the first Isle of Wight Arts Festival and founded, and now runs, The Tennyson Society. He was Chairman of the Island Arts Council until recently; his poetry is published by the Enitharmon Press, and his books about the Isle of Wight by Hammerton Book Services.

I *would* like to see another music festival here if it was properly controlled and planned. But it would have to be part of a whole Island festival and make the Isle of Wight to music what Edinburgh is to theatre. So you'd not just have pop music, but folk, classical and jazz, and use the whole Island. The pop festival would be part of the fringe which would then get the community on its side, rather than have local people think they're just being ripped off.

That's very much what I try to do with the arts. I ran the Arts Council here for the last seven or eight years and we did have a wider vision, which didn't always chime in with some of the local interests here. But look at Tennyson. He and his friends were considered quite dangerous by some people and probably resented. He was a controversial, rather miserable and aggressive figure, and didn't have a great deal to do with the local community except for opening Farringford once a year for the Flower and Produce Show. Two Americans went there one day, and told him they'd come all the way from America just to see him. And he said, 'It must not be, go back.' They went to see Mrs Cameron (the pioneer Victorian photographer), who lived just down the road in a house called Dimbola, and who was a friend of Tennyson's. She marched back with them to Tennyson and told him, 'They have come to see a lion and found a bear with a sore head. You must speak to them.' So in the end he was gracious!

Dimbola was recently saved from demolition by the strength of local feeling, sponsorship, a generous donation, grants and an interest-free loan. It is now a photographic museum. What we'd like to do is have contemporary writers, artists and photographers coming down to work there.

I want to make the Island a benchmark of artistic excellence again, a melting pot of ideas and influences. And also to attract people to the wonderful Victorian heritage we've got here. In Tennyson's time there were streams of visitors to Farringford, and to see Queen Victoria at Osborne House. I'd like to restore Freshwater as it was in those times, to have it ticking as a living centre for the arts. When we tried to have a Victorian

Festival, some people were very hostile and said, 'Oh, you mustn't look to the past'. But I say we can use the past to get back in touch with things like standards of excellence. People are so fixated – specially in the arts – about having to be politically correct, and the idea that one poem might be better than another is not allowed to be said. But unless you have high standards, you yourself can't try to attain them, and you end up patronizing people you're meant to be helping. I think you can learn a lot by looking backwards.

The Ghost Writer

At Christmas time journalists always scratch around looking for stories to fill the paper and one year I wrote about a haunted house near where I lived. People said it was really interesting and did I know such and such a place was haunted, and had I heard about the ghost of this and that? The Isle of Wight is a very haunted place and the stories were coming in so thick and fast that a sub-editor on the paper said we might have enough to make a little book. And we did one. *Ghosts of the Isle of Wight* came out in time for Christmas 1977 and we sold 3,000 copies in three weeks, which showed there was a market for it, though in those days it was difficult to persuade people to tell me their stories.

Gay Baldwin, 41, was born in Walsall, and came to the Island when she was 4. She has been a journalist on the *Isle of Wight County Press* for twenty-four years, does radio work and has published three books: *Ghosts of the Isle of Wight, More Ghosts of the Isle of Wight,* and *Ghosts of the Isle of Wight III*. She is married to David and they have one daughter.

The first book is still in print – 25,000 copies sold and still selling. There were about fifty stories in it, the more traditional ones, but many hadn't been written down before. There was a gap of fifteen years before the next book – I never was a speedy worker! When we moved to Cowes, my husband said it was about time I got busy on another one. I'd been collecting stories over the years and in January 1992 I started writing and got the book out in November with enough stories left over for book three. I've now sold about 35,000 copies in total.

I've really only scratched the surface and have more stories to research than I can possibly hope to get down. When people read one, they come to me with something they've experienced at the same place. Knighton Gorge is a good example: a manor-house which was demolished there in the 1800s is said to reappear on New Year's Eve. Islanders flock there to watch for it. Some say they see it and hear music.

Do I believe in ghosts? When I started I was sceptical, but the weight of evidence is such that there has got to be something. Too many people who are credible, rational and sensible have seen them. Quite often they say that when I have visited a house where a ghost has been reported, it becomes more active. Some people, I think, may make things up just to try to be in the book, but after about seventeen years of investigating hauntings, I can usually tell which those are, and I always want eye witnesses. Unless someone has actually seen the ghost, or heard or smelt it, I won't touch their story. I also try to speak to other people who have previously lived in the haunted property, and do a lot of research for historical detail. My books aren't just straight ghost stories.

In fact, this is how my ghost walks started. I'd written a ghost walk booklet you could use on your own, then I got some actors in Victorian costumes with top hats, morning coats and lanterns, to take groups around. It's the historical side we like to emphasize on the Newport walk and we're finding a lot of locals are coming in on it now.

I get stories from men and women, but women are often more willing to talk about ghosts. Men don't like to admit they've seen one. But it's now become acceptable not only to have seen one but to talk about it. I've never seen one myself, I'm someone with a journalistic background who is investigating. But I treat the stories very sensitively because people are giving me their name and reputation and on the Island everyone knows everyone. I still get excited when I hear a new one and I do like animal ghosts. I recently heard about a cat who died when its owners were on holiday, and they didn't have a chance to say goodbye. They were heartbroken, having had him for eighteen years. The following Sunday, the lady was in bed when she felt the cat jump up. And for a moment, she said, she forgot it had died. Then it turned round as cats do, purring, and just went. She felt it had come to say goodbye.

The Gardener, Cook, Writer, Illustrator, Hotelier . . .

I learnt to cook when I lived in Mombasa as a child because my mother wouldn't learn Swahili. There was father giving his dinner parties for twelve to the Governor etc., and mother would tell the Africans what she wanted in English with a bit of Swahili thrown in, and of course they loved to play her up. I picked up Swahili in no time and used to explain what she wanted, so without realizing it I was learning how to cook.

In 1955 Peacock Vane was a dead-beat guest house. But it was a beautiful Regency building and after we decorated and refurnished it, we became known all over the world for our food. Everything was very simple because I insisted on doing dinner as if you were at a private house party. I did all the cooking until I got some staff and taught them how to do it.

Joan Wolfenden, 75, has lived on the Isle of Wight since 1955. On leaving school, she worked as her father's secretary for a few years, and met her husband in East Africa during the Second World War when they were both in the Army. She ran Peacock Vane Hotel for many years, and has since written and illustrated *Recipes to Relish*, *The Glory of the Garden*, *The Satisfaction of Stitchery*, *The Year from Yaffles*. She has two children and four grandchildren; her husband died twenty years ago.

I was quite pleased to settle down at that time and if you're open for dinner every night you meet the most fascinating people. I always remember watching Winston Churchill's funeral on the box and in the little group of people walking behind the coffin, there were very few I hadn't fed.

When Margaret Thatcher was Minister of Education, she was dining at Peacock Vane with her family and sent the plates back because they were cold. I always carved at the hot plate but that night we were serving a grill on a dish and it's much easier to pass cold plates than hot ones. When Margaret Thatcher said in a loud voice, 'My plate's cold', I went and got some hot ones and said to my husband, 'She'll go far'. She had the guts to complain, and I thanked her. I said I'd spent all my life swearing at the staff, but when someone from outside complains it's much more effective. I also remember when Christopher Cockerell and his team of boffins came to celebrate his inventing the hovercraft. At the end of the evening not one of them had a cheque book or a penny between them to pay the bill! When my husband died, I gave Peacock Vane to my son and he sold it about four years ago.

Now, my greatest joy is to be out here in the garden I've created, watching everybody go by. There's nothing like sitting down and thinking some peaceful thoughts. For my next book I've gathered up some little prayers and put them with the hours of the day, illustrated with the language of flowers. There are 700 flowers and I've tried to paint them all, but it will be another year before I finish it. The trouble with flowers is that if you miss them when they're in bloom, you have to wait another year to paint them.

The Cookery Writer

Angela Hewitt, 43, was born in Dudley near Birmingham, and was a library assistant, laboratory technician and beauty consultant before coming to the Isle of Wight in 1972. Here, she cooked in restaurants, guest houses and for Brading Haven Yacht Club before opening her own restaurant, Lugleys, in Newport, which was mentioned in the *Good Food Guide*, *Egon Ronay* and won two AA rosettes. She closed the restaurant three years ago and now writes, illustrates and, with her husband Roger, publishes her own cookery books. These include: *Cooking on the Move*, *What's Cooking on the Isle of Wight?*, and *Isle of Wight Cookery*.

I've always been serious about cooking. My mother used to let me do it when I was very young, and my aunt in Birmingham ran a pork butchers where they made their own pies and sold butter loose by the pound. She'd let me play with the pastry and my uncle used to eat these dirty grey bits I'd cooked and say how wonderful they were.

The Isle of Wight is very much into promoting local food. The big thing is fish, particularly Bembridge prawns, though you can't get them every year. They look completely different from any other prawn, the veining is very orange, they're tiny, have a strong sea flavour, and Bembridge is the only place in the world they breed. They're farming oysters at Newtown Creek, there's garlic and sweetcorn, and I think the asparagus on the Island is the best in the world. Today's Mackerel Fayre is a resurrection of a medieval event. Just before the First World War, there were shoals of mackerel near Niton and the fishermen would just scoop them up. They don't come in shoals any more but eight years ago the Fayre was started again.

The Isle of Wight doughnut is mentioned in Eliza Acton's cookery books. It's small, about the size of a tangerine, and fried in lard so it's nice and greasy outside. Inside, the dough has to be stretchy rather than cakey and the orange peel and currants are tossed in cinnamon and sugar. A few years ago, there was only one company that made them and they closed down. I started writing about them and all of a sudden everyone's doing currant doughnuts again, so I'm really pleased.

I wouldn't say the Isle of Wight has the best cooks in the country, but I think we do have the best produce. There's lovely soil for arable crops and a climate a good two degrees warmer than the mainland. Everyone seems to have a garden growing something which they swap with neighbours. And if you drive along you see little benches outside houses with produce on them; you take what you want and put the money in a box.

The Crime Writer and Teacher

I think Island children are maybe more pleasant and malleable than I suspect mainland children are these days, and they do tend to look at the Island as the limit of their horizons. Sixth formers who apply to universities seem to want Portsmouth or Southampton – they're not longing to go far away, and a lot of them come back as soon as they can, and find jobs on the Island if at all possible. But unemployment here is the highest in the south. Yes, there is a drug buying problem, but we certainly don't have people selling them at the school gate. Most of it goes on on Ryde seafront where it's so easy for mainland dealers to come over from Portsmouth. But the police and drug prevention people here are very aware of it.

Mei Trow comes from the Rhondda Valley in Wales. He studied history at Kings College, London, gained a Certificate of Education at Jesus College, Cambridge, and taught in a Welwyn Garden City school before becoming head of history at Ryde High School. He has written two National Curriculum history books, fifteen crime fiction novels based on Conan Doyle characters, detective books set in a comprehensive school, and true crime books including one on the Craig/Bentley case (*Let Him Have it, Chris*). He has a regular local radio programme and has just ghosted a book on UFOs that will be published in June 1996. He is married to Carol, a hospital laboratory manager and Secretary of the Isle of Wight Music Festival, and they have one son.

I've been writing for ten years now and recently finished the second book in a series about a non-car-driving, bicycle-riding amateur detective who works in a comprehensive school. My colleagues say, is that me on page so and so? My deputy head is convinced he's in the book. He's not!

If you asked me ten years ago if I'd go back to the mainland, I'd have said, yes, like a shot. When we first came we weren't happy at all, it was a tremendous culture shock, like stepping back more than thirty years. But things have improved a lot since then and we've changed too. We're parents of an Islander – our son is one to his fingertips.

But . . . our library service is dreadful. Libraries close at five, don't have any specialist books, and you have to wait a very long time if you order something. I'd like to see them open every day until eight o'clock, Sunday as well, have a greater range of books, and a more welcoming atmosphere. The Lord Louis Library in Newport is a super building, but it has no loo, is as scruffy as hell on the outside and the stock is shambolic.

I'd like to see a purpose-built conference centre. I suppose the council would say there's no call for it, but if there was one, it might well be used. The Music Festival could be held there. At present it has to be in different buildings, there's nowhere big enough. We really need a university. Okay, we have Portsmouth, which is only 4 miles away, but that water might as well be the Pacific in terms of a psychological barrier.

The final thing we need which every other person will say we don't, is a bridge to the mainland. We've got to move into the twentieth century. There used to be a sign by the ferry saying 'Island roads are different'. They're not different, they're just archaic. When Queen Victoria was here, everything was here. *The Isle of Wight Connection* is a book I want to write one day. Karl Marx came, Tennyson and Liszt – in fact Liszt performed in a pub in Ryde in 1840. The place was humming then. Today, Islanders are very laid back. Some shops still close for lunch, by 4 o'clock they're winding down, polishing the floor. In a certain chain of coffee shops there are no cakes left after 2 o'clock. That's rather strange on a holiday island.

We're really out of touch with what's happening in the rest of the country. In terms of crime, of course, that's marvellous. But it's a two-edged sword.

For all that, I can't really see us going back to the mainland and settling in somewhere built up. This is a very beautiful place to live.

The Primary School Teacher

There is just myself and the Head Teacher, Helen Flynn, here at present and we have thirty-seven children aged five to nine in two classes. I have seventeen in my class this term – five boys and twelve girls – and you get a very close relationship not just with them, but the whole school and the parents as well. It's like an extended family.

We have beautiful surroundings with the sea not far away and are very hot on environmental studies. We run a Garden Club – quite a number of children stay after school

Janet Gallop, 57, was born on the Island in the house in Wroxall where she now lives. At 18 she went to a teachers' training college in south-east London, and taught in a primary school near the New Forest before going out to teach the children of British Forces serving in Germany and Aden. She came to Chale Church of England Primary School in 1967.

for that – and we're always walking out into the area to look at the flowers and trees and the birds. We also major on the history of this little place. Two years ago we had our 150th anniversary, and had a special day when we all dressed up in Victorian clothes. The building dates from 1843, but the school began across the fields before that.

Sometimes, our numbers have gone right down to twenty-four children, but we've managed to stay open. Nowadays, we control our own budget and if we can stay within it, we can stay open. In some respects this is a good idea, but it does make a lot of work for the Head and governors. In a small school you have to do everything.

You do notice mainland children when they come to the school. They are noisier, they've come from bigger classes, and they haven't always got the gentler characteristics that an Island village child might have, though I must say this does depend on their home backgrounds. Some who come from broken homes, and sadly we have a large number of them on the Island now, do have problems.

There are five village schools on the Isle of Wight and we're in a federation known as WASPS (Wight Association of Small Primary Schools). We are one of the smallest, but we all have around thirty children.

When I first came here we had a very close-knit community, and when we went on a school trip, most of the village came with us. We would hire a couple of coaches and go to the mainland. Now we go to places like

Osborne House or Carisbrooke Castle, the beach, or Parkhurst Forest, depending on the topic we're studying. But we aren't as close-knit a community as we ought to be, and the school is trying to foster stronger links with the village. On a Wednesday evening, we have a family games night which is open to everyone whether the children come here or not. At first, quite a lot of families came. Now I think parents like to let their children come and they can have a quiet night in. We have football, cricket, rounders, badminton, table tennis, and have just acquired a billiard table. One of the mums runs a French Club and some parents help with a Craft Club I run in winter. I teach children to knit. Grannies knit, but it seems that mums don't, and I feel the art isn't being passed down. This grieves me as I do a lot myself, so I thought I should start the children off, and we had quite a success last year with two or three boys coming in too.

I'm also working hard on the school garden – it's half an acre – because I want it to be a real place of interest for succeeding generations. We're putting in plants that attract butterflies and birds, and flowers you can smell and taste. We've tried sunflowers but they don't always grow that tall because the prevailing winds blow them over. But we have beans, tomatoes and marrows and the children can take home what they grow, so they go off proudly, with a marrow or lettuce under their arm.

I enjoy every aspect of teaching because I so love children. To me teaching is a calling. I feel God has put a love in my heart for them and we do our best to make this a happy place. I dread retiring but there are lots of things I want to do.

Matthew Tylor, 59, spent two years in the Royal Hampshire regiment in Malaya, and then read law at Southampton University. He entered Quarr Abbey, a Benedictine monastery near Ryde, when he was 24 and is now the Guest Master.

The Monk

Quarr Abbey was founded by French Benedictine monks when they were forced by the French government to leave France early this century. There were about a hundred here then, but they were able to return to France in 1922, earlier than expected, leaving behind twenty-five brothers to form this new community. We have carried on from them, though there are only about twenty-three of us now, which is an uncomfortably small number for such a large building. We also have 180 acres and let out the fields on short leases.

What any monk is trying to do, really, is search for God, live a life of prayer, and that's it, full stop. Everything else we do is to support that aim in study and work. The study concentrates on scripture, liturgy, church history and so on. We begin our day at 5.30 a.m. with the Office of Vigil – psalms, a hymn, a reading from the scriptures – and this lasts about three-quarters of an hour. Lauds is at 7 o'clock followed by an hour for spiritual reading, with Mass at 9 o'clock. During the morning we're doing work of one sort or another until the midday office. Dinner is at 1.15, recreation until 2.30, then more work. At 4.30 there's another short office and Vespers at 5 o'clock. After that most of the monks will be doing rather lighter things like writing letters. Supper is at 7.30 followed by a period of recreation, night prayers at 8.30, and then to bed. It's a long carefully structured day and, for a small community running a large monastery with a fair number of elderly people needing to be looked after, and youngsters being trained, a very busy one.

The youngest monk here now is in his early 20s. We don't like people coming in under 21, and they're usually in their early 30s. I think it's more difficult today for people to make up their minds. They change jobs more, marriage and divorce has changed radically from the 1950s, and these things affect monastic vocations as well.

We have about ten rooms where we can have men to stay, but women aren't allowed as they cannot come into the refectory where we eat. They can go to our sister house, St Cecilia's Abbey in Ryde. As Guest Master, I welcome the guests, explain when and where to turn up for meals, and then more or less leave them to it. I'm around the whole time, socializing with them, so if they want to talk they can. All sorts of people come. The biggest groups are social workers, male nurses and school teachers, but we also get barristers and solicitors. They're mostly Catholic, but not all. We have had Buddhist monks. There's no charge for guests but they usually leave a contribution, or help with the work if they can't afford to pay. If I'm asked what they should leave, I say £10 to £12 a day, and people are very generous.

We have a fortnight's holiday a year and stand in for parish priests on the Isle of Wight if they are called away in an emergency, but not for holidays or conferences. I have mixed feelings about being away. It is a change, but life here is very full.

I know it's a strange way to talk nowadays, but if one really believes in God with one's whole heart, loves Him and wants to serve Him, this is a fantastic life. It's also a very frustrating business, rather like painting. You never quite catch what you're trying to, but it's the ultimate thing about existence. I realize if someone doesn't believe in God, Christ and the Church, this life must appear absolutely bananas, idiotic beyond belief. But for me, serving Him with one's brethren is the most fulfilling thing I am capable of. I enjoyed reading law, it's a fascinating subject because you are up against human nature in its crises, and I went into it because I felt I could leave the world a better place than I found it. Litigation is a very human thing, but it dies with the litigant, and you can only do so much. What we're trying to do here is work for something that will last for ever.

Jane Newman, 40, came to the Isle of Wight ten years ago from Farnham, Surrey, where she'd been working in marketing and public relations. Her first job on the Island was at the Garlic Farm, where she advised on marketing, and she then joined the newly formed Rural Community Council in 1989. She is now its Deputy Director, an Honorary Director of the Isle of Wight Charitable Trust and on the regional advisory panel for the national lottery charities board, representing the voluntary sector in the south-east region. She is divorced and has two daughters.

The Community Fund-Raiser

When I saw an advertisement for a new organization called the Rural Community Council (RCC), I must confess I thought it was something to do with planting trees, and I've been trying to dispel that myth to everyone else ever since! In fact, it's an umbrella organization for all the charity and voluntary agencies on the Island and there are more than 1,000 of them. Our work is to make community development happen, not only by helping individuals have a better quality of life, but by making sure that development is done on a proper scale. Most people have the skills they need but not the knowledge or confidence to apply them. That's where we can help. In the last financial year the RCC brought in somewhere in excess of £600,000 to the Island to support charities here.

The Charitable Trust was formed two years after the RCC and has gone from strength to strength. Any voluntary or charitable agency or anyone with philanthropic aims can apply to it for a grant, providing they are on the Island. We raise funds through the Great Wight Walk every August – over £2,500 this year – a big auction, and through a membership drive with concessionary prices from Wightlink ferry. Unfortunately, a change of Wightlink ownership has meant we were not able to do it again this year (1995) but two-thirds of those who became members, have subscribed again. The Trust is also here to help self-help groups that don't know where they can get money from and can't afford to employ staff.

We have such a level of expertise here, that no matter what somebody comes to us for, we can provide what they want. There's twelve of us, but only three are full-time. We are supported by the Rural Development Commission, the Isle of Wight Council, and other sources we apply to. There are two specific project staff, externally funded, but managed by us, specializing in child care and social transport. Our rural officer deals with our parish councils and village halls and can give legal and financial advice.

We have a network of 100 voluntary drivers and if someone can't get access to public transport because of disability or finance, we can supply a driver to take them to a doctor, a friend, or just to see the scenery. The charge is 25p a mile, but we have a welfare fund and can pay for those in severe hardship. We want to make the scheme accessible to everyone. We've done a lot of research into what elderly people really want, not what others perceive they want: we asked individuals what kind of services they were missing, and a lot said transport. But we also discovered many living on their own with no close relatives were actually quite happy. Something they really wanted was chiropody. If their feet were better they could walk further.

We get a lot of politicians coming to the Island, but they're always shown the nice parts, so they're convinced we don't have any social problems. But we do. There *is* very high unemployment here, and we have the lowest male income in the country, some £39 less than the next one up. We also have the lowest gross domestic product of anywhere other than Greece in the whole of Europe, so you're talking about a very impoverished island. What I'd like visiting politicians to see are the projects that are grossly underfunded like the Womens' Refuge, Relate, and Challenge & Adventure organized originally by the police in conjunction with young offenders. We don't have massive crime here, but we're trying to address the problem before young people get to it.

The national lottery *has* made an impact in terms of people putting money into tins in the local shop. But it will take some time before this is felt. But we have been lucky. We've just received a grant from the lottery of an annual £18,000 to be paid over the next three years, and, of course, we're absolutely delighted about this.

The Governor of Parkhurst Prison

Max Morrison, 51, was born in Rochdale, Lancashire. He took a degree in social science and intended to be a teacher but saw an advertisement for assistant governors in the prison service and thought he'd 'give it a try'. He joined the service in 1967 and worked as a housemaster at Dover Borstal, at Blundeston in Suffolk, and for five years as Deputy Governor in Cardiff Prison. In 1975 he became Deputy Governor at Parkhurst, transferring in 1980 to London headquarters to work on a project dealing with violent and difficult prisoners. He became Governor of Camp Hill Prison in the Isle of Wight, went back to London headquarters to be in charge of physical security, and was then made Governor of Albany Prison on the Isle of Wight. Two years later, in January 1995, he was appointed Governor of Parkhurst.

One of the things in the prison service is that we've seen it all before at one stage or another, and we swing from being tough to being liberal and then go through it all again. At the end of the day, I suppose, this reflects the divided public opinion between those who would like to see much more caring reforming regimes, and the men on the Clapham omnibus who say 'Lock them up and throw away the key'. Somehow we've got to get the balance right.

Of course, you're occasionally going to get it wrong and someone out in the community on home leave will commit an offence. But the hysteria whipped up by newspapers and the media actually means home leave has now become politically unacceptable. This is a great loss because prisoners are part of society too, and at the end of the day, that's where they'll go when they're released. There is another side to it, too: some prisoners *are* going out and committing crimes, and that's a problem we find difficult to address because we can only judge them by what we see in prison, not how they behave when they're outside. But in this business you've got to take risks.

Parkhurst prisoners in the main are serving between five years and life. Some have been in the system for thirty years. I was somewhat chastened when I returned here in January and one said to me, 'Hello, Mr Morrison, nice to see you back'. I recognized him and said, 'What have you been doing?' bearing in mind it was eleven years since I'd been Deputy Governor here. He replied, 'Oh, I've been here.' That was quite frightening. People talk about long sentences but they don't understand the implications.

The staff are immensely capable of coping with incredibly aggressive, difficult and demanding prisoners. They can talk them down when many would be running away because they (the prisoners) are so angry. These are the skills we must keep intact. We tend to be a bit macho sometimes, but it's pretty disturbing for anyone to go into a cell where someone has been stabbed, committed suicide, or when they've been assaulted themselves.

Our Care Team try and pick up this kind of thing within twenty-four hours of an incident happening. My belief is that you can only create things out of a well-managed and controlled system, and that's what we're working on at the moment. We're developing active programmes which challenge people's offending behaviour, deal with their anger and the range of problems that cause them to offend. We have a special Unit C wing which takes the most difficult people in the prison system, the most dangerous, most violent and disturbed. It's highly staffed and supported by a psychologist, psychiatrist and prison staff, and does a tremendous job. There are prisoners here who have probably been in every other prison in the system; who have murdered other prisoners; who are so dangerous and so violent that staff are very, very wary of handling them in a normal location. And there's a possibility in the near future we will be able to develop another similar unit for equally difficult prisoners who need a different kind of treatment. What we want is somewhere where people are not going to be locked up for twenty-three hours a day, but don't have total free run of the prison. It should be a structured small unit where people who have tremendous problems with social skills can learn to develop them.

Most of the time, the three prisons on the Isle of Wight are welcome here and from the Island's point of view, there's a heck of a lot of money going into the community from them. I guess this prison alone is pushing about £13 million a year, and the other two about £14 million between them. An awful lot of people benefit from this apart from prison officers spending their wages. There's food, transport and other services bought locally. I think if the prisons left the Island, the Island would be devastated. We must be one of the largest employers. We have over 500 staff, Albany has 300 and Camp Hill nearly 300.

The Chancellor of the Exchequer has made it fairly clear that public expenditure has to be reduced and I can't ignore this. The frustrating thing is that there is so much here I'd like to do, but it all costs money. I sometimes think I could just afford a certain initiative because of careful husbandry, and then I'm told, 'Ah, but actually we want you to *reduce* your budget'. They say people want to pay less income tax. I think they'd rather have better services.

I'm not sure prison in itself can do anything to reform anybody. That has to come from the individual. What we can do is provide the skills which are very often missing – educational, work, social, anger management – to give the prisoner the best chance when he gets out. Some of them have tremendous skills deficits, but if you look at their records you see truanted from school, broken home, abused or subject of violence. It's hardly surprising most of them are what they are. If you want to break the chain, you must deal with the family as a unit when the children are quite small – the parents have much to learn as well.

I certainly think too many people are sent to prison. I'm not saying there isn't a good case for it. Society needs to be protected and prison is a perfectly viable way of dealing with some offenders. But in the main it's very expensive, terribly disruptive to families, and doesn't really help the offender. The problem is, we don't have enough alternatives in this country. We should have workshops, tailor-made schemes for offenders in the community, maybe even compulsory education. A lot of prisoners have problems with reading, writing and arithmetic though it's difficult to sell this kind of education to fairly tough individuals. But you can teach basic skills through a variety of media. There's a real need to move to a more coherent core curriculum of English, Information Technology and Maths. One of the problems is that prisoners start doing a course at one prison, get moved to another, and find there's a different syllabus. We're trying to get a system now so they can continue a course wherever they are and gain accreditations they can carry with them.

I came here on 16 January after three prisoners escaped. I know what I saw on that date, and I know where we're going now. Prisoners couldn't get into workshops as a result of the escape, control had broken down. I've never experienced anything quite so awful in my life. You went into a wing and there'd be sixty prisoners all hanging around complaining, and the staff were totally overwhelmed. We regained control with difficulty and it was a pretty hairy period, almost like an institutional nervous breakdown. Everything had just fallen apart. But we have made enormous changes and in August, there was suddenly a sea change. People were saying, 'My God, it's better.' It's not me. The staff have done marvels.

There's always a balance to be maintained in a prison between prisoners and staff. If prisoners get too much freedom, life is made difficult for the staff. My objective is to make life better for the staff, because I believe that if *they* feel confident and are firmly in charge, then good things can happen to prisoners. But it should be in a structured way rather than just allowing freedom. Prisoners who have been very dangerous criminals outside don't stop being dangerous because they're in prison.

The Home Secretary has given some prisoners natural life sentences which means they are going to spend the remainder of their life in prison. I disagree with this. I think you have to give people hope, something to work for, and you've also got to believe people can change. I wouldn't have any purpose in working in the prison service if I didn't believe, though not for religious reasons, in the power of redemption, that people can actually say, 'I made a mistake in my life, I atoned for it, and now I want to live differently'. If you give someone a natural life sentence, it's denying him that and if you're just going to lock him up and cage him for the rest of his life, it's almost worse than the death penalty.

In December 1995 Parkhurst Prison was downgraded to a category B despite deputations to the Home Secretary Michael Howard requesting that it be kept as a top security prison. The downgrading followed the recommendation of the Learmont Report published earlier in the year, but ignored the fact that since that time (and since the escape of the three prisoners in January 1995), several million pounds had been spent on upgrading security, and most other recommendations had already been implemented.

The Prison Officer

Marie Young, 28, comes from Donegal and studied ecology at the University of Ulster in Northern Ireland, where she met her husband Brian. In 1988 they worked in Iceland for six months, came to London and Marie applied for a job in the prison service at a job centre because, she says, it was the highest paid job going. She is now a prison officer at Camp Hill Prison, where Brian also works.

I began my training at the height of the Strangeways riots in 1990 and people thought I was mad. But I was at Wakefield for nine weeks and that made you feel quite confident about the work you had to do.

There are now about a dozen women prison officers to 120 male officers at Camp Hill and probably about the same in the other two prisons on the Island (Albany and Parkhurst). Five years ago there was only myself and another girl, and a lot of staff tended to resent women. But after I'd been here six months, one of the blokes called me into his office and said he had to apologize for his attitude at the start. He said he now had no problems and no fears that I wasn't capable of doing the job. Women are now fully accepted, but I've had a couple of bad moments I didn't expect from some of the older staff. We now have a women's group that meets every three months. We get together in confidence and discuss any problems we might have.

Camp Hill is an all-male prison with sentences of four years or less. Prisoners can't have open conditions, but don't need the maximum security of a Category A or B prison. They're mainly in for drugs, car theft, burglary. We get a lot down from London as well as locally. Most of them are very young, the average age is about 24, and their outlook very immature. They do try it on with us at the start thinking, 'Oh, she's a woman, she must be a soft touch, we can get anything we want from her'. They generally find we're more strict than the other officers, and they soon realize they're not going to get away with anything, and turn to you as someone to talk to. I think they're more relaxed in our company. And it's also said if a female is on the wing, it's less tense. We tend to bring a bit of sanity to a stressful situation.

I work in the library which at one time was a job for someone about to retire. Luckily we had a change of governor and he decided he wanted people to use it for more than just exchanging books. We now have about 90 per cent of the 400 inmates at Camp Hill coming through a week, so we're quite pleased with that. But I still have wing-based duties, I unlock inmates and give them their breakfast and lunch, unlock them again after lunch, get them out to work, see them back in again for tea, and then unlock them again for association in the evening. This is when they can have a shower, watch TV, play darts or make a phone call. I'm also a Legal Aid officer and can direct people where they should go for help. We run a Citizens' Advice Bureau one afternoon a month, and inmates go there with any problems I can't deal with.

A lot of prisoners will tell you they're going to go straight, but there is quite a high re-offending rate in the whole of the prison service. It's quite sad when an old face comes back in. You do feel you've failed. When you meet ex-inmates in the street, you don't know how they will react to you. Mostly it's favourably, but you have to expect adverse reaction. I greet them, it's no good ignoring them. The problem is not going to go away and you'll probably see them again. Sometimes they'll come up to you and show you the little baby they've just had, or tell you how they're getting on, and that's really nice. We go down to the town to deal with newspaper orders on Fridays, and I've been asked where the nearest car park is because people think I'm a traffic warden or a policewoman. When I tell them I'm a prison officer, they say, 'You don't look like one'. They expect us to be large and round but none of us at Camp Hill are like that.

Last year I treated Brian to a holiday on Jersey for his birthday and we spent an afternoon at the Shire Horse Centre. He came back and said, 'I'm going to have a shire horse', booked himself on a heavy-horse handling course and now we have four horses and have started doing wagon rides through the forest and log-pulling for the Forestry Commission.

The horses have a wonderful temperament, soft as butter. I ride some of them as well, and just to be out in the forest with a shire, on its back or on a wagon, is just . . . wonderful. They're always pleased to see you. I go out to them first thing in the morning before I go to work and say 'good morning' and they come up for a pat, and it just sets you up lovely for the day. You go into work and feel less aggrieved. The inmates can bring on anything they want and you know you can go back out in the evening and see the horses again, and just let all your problems drop.

The Prison Visitor

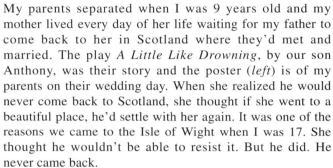

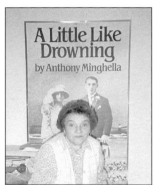

Gloria Minghella was born in Leeds. As well as working with her husband in their ice-cream business, she was a founder member of the Isle of Wight Citizens' Advice Bureau and is now its President. She is President of the Ryde Carnival, the oldest carnival in England, and Chairman of the Isle of Wight Housing Trust. She was elected to Medina Borough Council when her husband retired, and became its first Lady Mayor. She has been a Deputy Lieutenant of the Island for ten years and a magistrate for fifteen. She is married to Edward (see page 67) and has five children and eight grandchildren.

My parents separated when I was 9 years old and my mother lived every day of her life waiting for my father to come back to her in Scotland where they'd met and married. The play *A Little Like Drowning*, by our son Anthony, was their story and the poster (*left*) is of my parents on their wedding day. When she realized he would never come back to Scotland, she thought if she went to a beautiful place, he'd settle with her again. It was one of the reasons we came to the Isle of Wight when I was 17. She thought he wouldn't be able to resist it. But he did. He never came back.

It wasn't until our oldest daughter was going to university that I realized I hadn't got a life outside the family and our ice-cream business. I'd always wanted to be involved with people so I wrote to the Governor of Parkhurst Prison and said I'd like to be a prison visitor. I got a reply saying there wasn't a provision, but if I wanted to help, there were other jobs I could do. After a bit of vetting, I was invited to be on the Associate Probation Service. My job was to collect mums and wives from the ferry, take them to the prison, and bring them back. Eventually I was able to work inside, and spent the next ten years with the three prisons here: Parkhurst, Albany and Camp Hill. I used to think if I could make prisoners think differently, that would improve their quality of life, and if I could improve that, someone else's life outside would be better, too.

For one who suffers from claustrophobia, I found it surprisingly easy to go into the prisons, simply because when I was there I was focusing on the other person. Many didn't want to see me to start with. I represented, not the establishment, but a kind of reflection of their conscience. Then they realized I was not forbidding or judgemental. Often they tried to disarm me by saying they were atheists or agnostic. I'd say, that's fine, that's not part of the deal. One man (he has since died) had murdered his child. He wanted to tell me everything. I said I didn't want to know. Our friendship was not conditional on whether he was sorry or not sorry. When prisoners realized this, I made a lot of good friends and found the whole thing very rewarding.

I always say it's very easy to do the right thing when everything's going for you, when there's enough food in the larder, and when someone cares about you. What is hard is when you have none of these things. I feel there is some good in every soul in this world.

I felt, tremendously, the burden of being the first Lady Mayor here, and wanted so much to make a good job of it and not let women down. The welfare and prosperity of the Borough has always been important to me. Edward and I both have a genuine feel for the place that's given us the chances we've had, and if we have something we can do or give, we always do.

The Police Superintendent

I have 206 police officers, including the drug squad, communications and traffic staff, and although we are self-sufficient to some extent, we do occasionally have to call police in from the mainland. No small police unit today can operate alone. When three prisoners escaped from Parkhurst in January 1995, hundreds of officers were called over from the mainland, and others came over in 1994 when we had the fire bombings in Newport and Ryde by the animal liberation people. We have extra officers in during Cowes Week, too. But we would deal with a murder case ourselves unless it was a major one.

Travelling and communications are our biggest problems. The roads are so narrow that everybody goes at the speed of the slowest driver. I remember the first time I went out to an injury accident at Yarmouth. We had our blue lights flashing and came up behind the proverbial green mini driven by a little old lady who didn't see us. We were actually driving to an injury accident at 25 miles an hour.

Superintendent Alan Emmott, 49, comes from Hampshire and went into the police force straight from school. He worked in various police stations before coming to the Isle of Wight in August 1994. He is married to Margaret, who is Head Teacher of a Portsmouth school and commutes daily.

Surprisingly, we are the fourth busiest custody centre in Hampshire Police, and have more prisoners going through this station (we have eight cells) than all but three other stations. Yet when you look at the crime rate per population, we have one of the lowest in the country, and the quality of life is high. People proudly come up to me and say they don't lock their doors when they go out. But there were 709 burglaries last year (1994), and 15 per cent were walk-ins through the back door. We've tilted our resources over this last year trying to detect household burglaries. Arresting those who have committed the offences is usually down to informants and burglar alarms.

We have a number of country beat officers who work in rural areas and live in a police house. But we can't have all police officers walking the beat. We try to find a balance according to circumstances. We wouldn't want too many around pub closing times, for instance, because this could inflame a situation. And is this an efficient way to use a very expensive resource? Hampshire Police now has a bottom line budget of £165 million and our finances come out of that money.

I don't think we have a big drugs problem here though we did have an increase in offences last year. But that was because we had a particular push on them – if we don't go and look for them we haven't got a problem. We can only be hit by our own statistics. People say the drugs problem has gone up dramatically here. It hasn't, and the link between drugs and burglary hasn't been proved. We do have people using amphetamines, ecstacy and cannabis, which is part of society now. We find cannabis is grown here rather than bought in concentrated form, because people just haven't got the money. We don't turn a blind eye to it – research has shown that taking cannabis over many years does adversely affect the brain, and is more dangerous for pregnant women than tobacco.

Drink driving is not a horrendous problem here. People do speed a bit, and we have a radar team from the mainland for the roads we think are the most problematic. Then we'll probably get about seventy or eighty speeding over a week. It's the same as the mainland, but we only have half a mile of dual carriageway.

One of the main things I've tried to do here is encourage community policing in relation to Neighbourhood Watch and we are forming an association which will administer itself. I think this is a way of enhancing a community spirit and thereby people's quality of life. Statistics put out by General Accident certainly show it does reduce crime.

The Magistrate

I very quickly realized that although being a farmer's wife was extremely fulfilling, I needed to do something else as well. So when I was asked to join the Bench, I jumped at the chance. We used to sit in Benches of five, with the most senior in age taking the chair. Being very young I would be stuck out at the end, and usually the decisions had been made before I ever heard what was going on.

It's very different nowadays. Magistrates are highly trained for the first three years and even then we carry on having refresher courses. At the moment we have twenty-seven women and thirty-eight men – a company director, a bus driver, electrician, teacher, shop keeper, boatbuilder, me a farmer's wife. . . . The most common crimes we have are petty theft and traffic offences. We don't have people breaking the 70 mile an hour limit, of course, but we do have them breaking the 30 mile an hour limit through the villages.

Because it's a holiday island, we attract holiday workers and quite a number turn up in court for burglary and theft. And there's a little knot of Island people as well. One of the worrying aspects of crime here is the increase in public order offences caused through alcohol, just late night fracas, bad language and shouting outside pubs and in town centres. We have the highest unemployment rate in the south-east region, but I'm not sure this should be directly related to public order offences.

I think it's up to the Chairman of the Magistrates to present a good image to the public and this is something I've tried to do. We've just got a project off the ground, where magistrates go into schools to raise children's awareness of the work we do. We're really aiming at the 14-year-olds so we can get through to them hopefully before they start offending.

Judi Griffin, 53, was born in Oxfordshire and came to the Isle of Wight when she was 7. Her parents ran a bicycle and toy shop in East Cowes. She worked in the Civil Service and as Bursar's Secretary at Bembridge School before marrying Richard, a farmer. They have five children and two grandchildren. She has been a governor of a Catholic middle school, became a magistrate when she was thirty, and is now Chairman of the Bench, the first woman to hold the appointment. She was on the Board of Visitors at Camp Hill Prison for fourteen years, is a Deputy Lieutenant and in 1996 will become High Sheriff.

It *can* be difficult for a magistrate living in a small community, but when we look through our morning list and see a name we recognize, we just stand down. What's more likely to happen is that we don't actually know the name of the person and in will come the chap from down the road.

Worried parents come to me from time to time to ask me about procedures, but no one has tried to use me to influence sentences. I tell them about the process of law. I can take them into the court room, for instance, and let them see what's going on. We had an open day earlier this year (1995), the first of its kind on the Island, and one of the first in the country. We had 600 people through on the Saturday. They wanted to know how we became magistrates, who we were, what we did.

We have our own penalties committee here that looks at national guidelines for magistrates and adapts them to suit the Island. In fact, I think we were awarding more community service orders than any other part of the country at one time and must have had a high rate of success otherwise we wouldn't have carried on doing it.

I spent fourteen years working as a volunteer on the Board of Visitors at Camp Hill Prison. We don't befriend prisoners as prison visitors do. We're a group of people who have the right to go anywhere we want within the prison and speak to anyone we want to at any time, with access to the Secretary of State.

Being Chairman of the Magistrates *was* a daunting task to take on and I thought, 'Golly, I don't know if I can deal with this'. But I wanted to have a go. My background is very humble and I think if my father could see me now he'd say, 'Blow me tight, look at Judi'.

The Lady Reeve

Five years ago, some friends, a former High Sheriff and his wife, asked my husband if he'd like to be High Sheriff. We were absolutely flabbergasted and said, 'No, we couldn't possibly'. But we thought about it for a week, and decided it would be an amazing thing to do. Moneywise it is expensive, but it's a tremendously great honour to represent Her Majesty the Queen on the Island for a year. So we said we'd love to do it. John's name was put forward to Her Majesty who, so they say, has to choose one of several names, with a golden bodkin.

I wasn't sure I was going to like being a public figure. John is a very calm person, takes everything very much in his stride, I'm a great worrier. But having been the High Sheriff's wife now for a few months, I absolutely love it. My duties are to be with John on every occasion when he's out and about, which is quite often. I have to be not exactly at his side, but a few steps back. It has amazed us both to see how much goes on on the Island. We didn't have a clue before. We were in agriculture and one doesn't perhaps see much beyond that.

John has an amazing outfit which you can buy from another sheriff. It's a black velvet double-breasted jacket with large buttons that look like diamonds, a lace ruff round the neck, black velvet knickerbockers, buckled shoes, a tricorn hat and sword. On his Declaration Day, it took the family about two hours to get him dressed. I now keep all the gear in a spare room, so if we're called on suddenly, everything's there.

He had only been High Sheriff for a fortnight when we had the Duke of Kent here as president of the RNLI. We had to have a chauffeur for the visit, but didn't know where to get one from, so we asked our herdsman who knows the Isle of Wight like the back of his hand – his family have been here for generations – if he'd be chauffeur for the day. He said he'd love to and took to it like a duck to water.

The High Sheriff's wife doesn't have any traditional clothes, but I do have a title. A lot of people at functions come forward and say 'How do you do, Lady Reeve'. I was really surprised the first time. Before John became High Sheriff, I was very apprehensive about meeting lots of people, but I've surprised myself. I don't know whether it's sent from above, but something has certainly happened for me to cope with it all and it's opened our eyes to how many people on the Island give their whole lives to so many causes – it makes me feel very humble.

['Reeve' comes from the Anglo-Saxon 'gerefa', an Old English word for magistrate. There were borough-reeves, port-reeves, etc. The sheriff (q.v.) is the shire-reeve.]

Sue Attrill, 54, was born on the Isle of Wight during the Battle of Britain. Her father was Robert Hodgson, the artist, and the family later lived in Yorkshire and Kent. At 17 she worked as a nanny in Turkey and London before returning to teach in a kindergarten at Seaview. She now lives in a large farmhouse that has been in her husband, John's, family for generations, and lets out part of it to holiday-makers. She has worked with the NSPCC and on church committees. John, a farmer and Master of the Isle of Wight Hunt, has recently been appointed High Sheriff of the Isle of Wight. They have two grown-up children and one grandchild.

The Governor

David, 4th Lord Mottistone, 75, was born on the Island. He went to Dartmouth Naval College at 13, and spent most of the Second World War in the Western Approaches. He retired from the Navy at his own request in 1967 because he disagreed with government defence policy to abolish aircraft carriers. He inherited the title when his immediately older brother died in 1966. (His eldest brother was killed in the First World War and another brother died in 1964.) He worked in industry (Radio Rentals, the Cake and Biscuit Alliance), became Lord Lieutenant of the Isle of Wight in 1986, and Governor in 1992. He has been involved with many Island and national charities and supports several in parliament. Mottistone Manor, where he spent much of his childhood, is now owned by the National Trust. He has been married to Anthea for fifty-one years. They have four children and fourteen grandchildren.

My great-grandfather, Charles Seely, had been sent to the Isle of Wight as a youth from his home in Lincolnshire where his father was a miller, to recover from an illness. One day he walked over the Downs and gazed out across beautiful green fields to a blue sea and said to himself, so my father told me, that when he made his fortune, he would own that land. When the family mill burnt down, he bought farmland in Nottinghamshire under which they fortuitously discovered a coal mine. By the 1840s he had made the fortune he needed to buy the land he wanted on the Isle of Wight. My father, the first Lord Mottistone, was given a peerage when he served in Asquith's cabinet before the First World War.

The Lord Lieutenant here has three main responsibilities: loyalty to the Crown, which includes looking after royal visitors when they come; chairing a committee which recommends magistrates to the Lord Chancellor; and support for the Territorial Army. Until 1974, the Lieutenancy was shared with Hampshire, and with the change in local government structure, some people said they'd like to make us a district of Hampshire. But that had been tried, unsuccessfully, in the 1880s. So a year later than everyone else, we were made a separate county. Then in 1972, the authorities said, rather stuffily, 'Well, if you are to remain a separate county, you'll have to have a separate Lord Lieutenant and High Sheriff', which we'd never had before. In 1992, on the fortieth anniversary of Queen Elizabeth's coronation, the Isle of Wight County Council proposed I should be appointed Governor. This was a particularly important honour to me because there have been Captains, Governors or Lords of the Isle of Wight since Norman times. My full title is now Governor, Captain and Steward.

Some people say the Island ought to be run like a large company. They don't realize it is an independent island as well as an essential part of English local government and it's not always easy to share activities with mainland bodies. Central government officials don't seem to understand this and find us maddening because we don't conform to what they think we ought to. When we say, look we *are* different, they say, yes, but that's superficial. But, it *is* important. The fact is, we live like we do because we want to live on an island, the only English island which is wholly a county in its own right and has been for over a hundred years. Officials fall over backwards to try and make everyone the same.

You occasionally get a minister to see our point of view, and the next thing you know he's been moved somewhere else. Civil servants sometimes understand it. But what matters is not what they think, but what is written in their paper work. On 'How to handle the Isle of Wight' for social services, it will read: 'Don't treat them differently'. By the time you've converted an official to our way of thinking, he's got moved on, so its a perpetual battle.

I think it would be jolly nice if a big company or government department was to set up a factory or office on the Island because unemployment is worse than anywhere else in the south of England. We do have a limited Assisted Area Status now, but it's nothing like as effective as the money Welshmen and Scotsmen were getting in the 1970s and later. What we want is for people who are thinking of setting up factories to see the Island as a good place to come to. That's the sort of thing I'm battling for all the time.

[Lord Mottistone retired as Governor and Lord Lieutenant in December 1995.]

The Councillors

Morris Barton: The local Council has been Liberal or Lib Dem controlled since 1981 and the Island had a Liberal Member of Parliament for many years until Stephen Ross had to retire through ill health in 1985. We are now a unitary authority and we campaigned for this almost since reorganization in 1974. Services for 123,000 people can easily be dealt with by one authority and it makes administrative sense both in Whitehall and Europe. On the Isle of Wight Council today, there are forty-eight councillors: 34 Lib Dems, 1 Independent Liberal, 5 Conservatives, 5 Independents, 3 Labour. We are

Morris Barton, OBE, 54, is a fifth-generation Islander, and his great-great-great-grandfather was one of the builders of Barton village, near Newport, which was named after him. Morris has always lived on the Island. He joined the Labour Party in 1959, was elected to the Council in 1969, joined the Liberal Party in 1976 when there was an influx of Labour Militants, and became Leader of the Council in 1982. In 1995 he took early retirement from the *Isle of Wight County Press* where he worked for thirty-nine years as compositor, proofreader and linotype operator. He was awarded the OBE for public and political services. He is married to Marcia and they have two daughters and three grandchildren.

responsible for all the services bar the police and the health trust.

I think the Island should be looked at in the way the Channel Islands and the Isle of Man are, and we should be given more freedom to run our own affairs. There should also be some appreciation of the fact that we are a retirement catchment area and we should get some assistance from the Department of Health for supporting elderly people. Some 23 per cent of our population is over the age of 65 and that, of course, leads to greater dependency on social services and community care. But we have a budget that relates to a land-locked English county and makes no allowance for the fact that we're an island. The Department of Environment doesn't recognize there is such a thing as an English island.

We have a huge unemployment problem – it's always hovering between 11 and 15 per cent. In some areas in the recent recession, it was up to 25 per cent. We've always kept a balance between manufacturing industries and tourism, but the manufacturing side has been affected by the recession. Tourism has held up reasonably well, but that doesn't provide long-term employment and allow people to invest in homes. What we'd like to encourage is high tech manufacturing industries to come here. We should be saying to them, 'Look, if you come to the Isle of Wight, there are lots of advantages outside the question of severance by sea. There is good education for children, and quality of life for families, it's relatively crime-free, its natural attractions are abundant.'

But when mainland companies look at relocation, they see the cost of the ferries, and as we're not recognized as a development area, or a European Objective Zone, we are very low in the league tables in terms of being an attractive investment area. Our GDP is lower than anywhere in the country apart from one Welsh county and Northern Ireland. We should be trying to get funding from both UK government and Europe as an area in need of particular assistance.

Our aim on the Council is to bring down the cost of the ferries and have some local input into the cross-Solent carriage market. The cost is out of all proportion, but the government is not prepared to provide transport subsidies. I think some at least should be given to businesses.

One thing I do despair of is that Islanders tend to talk the Isle of Wight down. Ideas are put up and they knock them down immediately, so nothing happens. But if we are going to move into the next century with some optimism, people have got to be prepared to face change. At the moment we are putting forward a number of ideas – a monorail system, a marina – not things that perhaps would fit in with the average Islander's view of life here, but things that are very necessary for jobs and the future. Even before a project is formulated, they say it's a waste of time, pie in the sky. The local press do that all the time. They seem to take the view that anything proposed by hoteliers, local authority or the tourist board is a waste of time before it gets anywhere. If we're all going to work together as a community we've got to have a much more positive up-front view of the Island and talk it up rather than down. I'd also like to see a more balanced community on the Island. Having, according to the 1991 census, 26.9 per cent of the population over pensionable age and a very small number of people employed, is not good for the future.

Our roads? We're moving towards a policy whereby we look at a map of future road schemes and wipe out as many as we possibly can in an effort to encourage people to use public transport. Then we will use the money we would have spent on road improvements, on cycle ways and improving public transport through concessionary fares.

I'm always optimistic. I wouldn't be involved in politics if I wasn't. I've had opportunities to further my political career in a number of directions but always felt this is the place I could do most good.

Valerie Anderson: One of our big problems is the gross under-funding of the Care in the Community Act. The Isle of Wight has a very high percentage of elderly people, with 23 per cent of our population over 65. In fact we're the second highest in the country for this age group, and the highest for over 85s. In the first year when we heard what our budget for Care in the Community was to be (£1,500,000) we were happy because it was sufficient. But the basis for the grants didn't suit London and a lot of

Valerie Anderson, 51, first came to the Isle of Wight twenty-eight years ago for a week-end break. She and her husband-to-be fell in love with it and decided to come and live here. In London she'd worked in a Merchant Bank; on the Isle of Wight she took a job in a coal merchant's office, and later ran a haberdashery and ladies' wear shop in East Cowes. She became Chairman of the Local Business Association and in 1985, standing as a Liberal, was elected to the Isle of Wight County Council. She was on the social services committee for ten years, a representative on the Association of County Councils for two years, and Chairman of the County Council until May 1995, only the second woman in 103 years to hold that position. She is now Chairman of the Financial Services and Contracts Committee. She is married to Sam and they have two sons.

metropolitan authorities, and the formula was changed. There's nothing in it now that recognizes the number of elderly people or the large number of residential homes we have here. We lost a great deal of money with the new formula and it hit our services quite badly.

The Isle of Wight County Council led the field in domiciliary services that enabled people to remain in their own homes for the maximum amount of time, but we now have to deal only with cases that have the most pressing needs, and are not able to do the preventative work we've done in the past. An independent company has now been formed called Isle Care which runs the former council homes and allows a greater level of investment and up-grading of facilities in them.

There is hidden homelessness. Very rarely do you see people in shop doorways, but what we do have is a floating population of youngsters who crash out in other people's homes and don't appear in the statistics. This particularly applies to 16–18 year olds who aren't eligible for unemployment or housing benefit. A lot take summer jobs with accommodation provided and at the end of the season don't want to leave the Island. If they're going to be unemployed, they probably feel they may as well be somewhere that's pleasant to live.

Another problem for young people is property prices. They're low compared to the mainland, but wages are low too and many can't afford to buy a house because they don't earn enough for a mortgage. Most of them, if they've got families, live at home. I think there should be more places to rent and rents should be lower. The average for what were former council stock and are now Housing Association houses, is £50+ a week. This is a large hole in the wage of someone only earning £7,000 a year, and many on the Island in full-time work do earn that kind of salary.

I'd like the local authorities to go back to being providers of housing, and given the funds to do it. Everything is now privatized or hived off, and councils are just there to vet contracts and make sure things are provided by somebody else, which I don't think always works for the benefit of the people.

There are all kinds of projects that have got planning permission but haven't got off the ground because of the recession. One of our schemes is for a 'foyer', in which young people can learn different skills with accommodation provided, as well as leisure and sporting facilities. This would be part of a composite scheme and I've got my eye on a field where a building could go.

One thing which is very good here is the relationship between the Council and voluntary sector. The Riverside Centre in Newport is funded by both. This is a place with all kinds of workshops, social facilities, a restaurant, classes in photography, computers, creative writing, repairing wheelchairs, aerobics, and many more. It is a place where people with physical and mental handicaps as well as the able-bodied can all meet together and members of the public are encouraged to buy from the workshops, have lunch and hire the building for functions. The place really buzzes.

I'm also very proud of the fact that social services started a company called Osel Enterprises for people with learning difficulties. It produces Wight Crystal bottled water which is far better than Perrier! They have a picture framing business, a small market garden which produces vegetables and flowers, and they sell plants to other Island nurseries. It gives proper employment rather than piece-work jobs and they're now bringing out a new drink called Kixse, a sweet, herbal cordial made in Newport many years ago. The recipe belongs to a local philanthropist who has given Osel the right to produce it.

The Music Administrator

I owe my music to my mother, she was an excellent accompanist. At 6 I was on the kitchen floor playing with two sticks and she said that meant I wanted to play the fiddle. And that's when I started. War came when I was 18, and there was an occasion in Burma when I had just left an observation post and within seconds the chaps who took over got a direct hit with a shell and were all killed. After that I've always thought life was a bonus, I've had my day and should give what I can to other people.

There was a lot of talent on the Island but it wasn't organized. A music teacher would say, 'Let's do something'. They'd do Benjamin Britten's *War Requiem*,

Norman Thurston, 74, was a Surveyor of Customs & Excise for forty-three years. He spent four years in Burma during the war, studied violin at the Royal College of Music, taught music in schools, was a founder member of the Forest Philharmonic Society Orchestra and the Stewart and Aurelian Quartets, and an executive of NFMS South Region. He 'retired' to the Isle of Wight in 1983 and became director and administrator of the Island's International Oboe Competition, Vice-president of the Island Symphony Orchestra, and music representative of the Healing Arts Steering Group at St Mary's Hospital. He teaches violin and viola. He is married to Jackie and they have three children and five grandchildren.

and anyone who wanted to play did. No one was ever paid, they just enjoyed themselves. In September 1983 two chaps came over from the Bournemouth Symphony Orchestra to act as peripatetic teachers, and they started up regular orchestral rehearsals. One of them was Neil Courteney, who now runs the music on the Island. When I was asked to be administrator of the Isle of Wight Symphony Orchestra, I said, in a rather big-headed sort of way, yes, but it would have to be done properly with high quality playing. The first year we had a turnover of £847 from four concerts; today, it is something in the region of £50,000.

We play in the Medina Theatre which has 430 seats but you can't market that number properly, and we are losing something like £3,500 a concert. What I'd really like is for the Isle of Wight Council for the Arts to produce a new multi-purpose hall at the Mountbatten Centre in Newport.

We need a bigger hall, too, for our oboe competition. The idea for that came in 1990 when I mentioned to Lady Barbirolli, the symphony orchestra's president, that we were thinking of getting a competition going. She said, 'For heaven's sake, don't make it a mixed one. You can't judge trumpets and harps and pianos together. But if you'd like to make it an oboe competition, I'll chair it free of charge.'

It took three years to get it started and we had our second one this year (1995). Lady Barbirolli comes over for it and we have judges and competitors from all over the world. There are several reasons for having the competition: to give a good opportunity to young oboe players up to 30 years of age; to help the economy of the Island; and to establish it in the international field.

What we don't have on the Island is a good music shop, and most of us have to go to the mainland when we want to buy some.

[Sadly, Norman Thurston died in September 1995.]

The Young Islanders

Matthew: The Isle of Wight is a very nice place to live, not as violent as the mainland. There's no shortage of things to do, but transport is a bit of a problem. If my parents don't

Matthew and Rachel Thomas were both born on the Island. Their parents, Roger and Ruth, moved here from Staffordshire fourteen years ago when Roger was offered a farm manager's job. He has since become a partner in the farm and is Chairman of the British Holstein Cattle Society. Matthew, 15, and Rachel, 14, both go to Ryde School. During the holidays, Rachel helps at a nearby farm shop; Matthew works in a pub.

take us somewhere, we have to be up and ready for the bus which is once an hour from here, so you have to plan ahead. But you get used to it. Ryde has most of the main attractions. It's got a bowling alley, skating rink and a beach. But the shops aren't as good as Newport. If I'm really desperate for something I can get on the hovercraft at Ryde and that's about ten minutes to Portsmouth. I've looked everywhere on the Island for trainers and there are none suitable. But that's not as big a problem as I'm probably making out.

The good things? The countryside is so pleasant. I cycle a lot and roads are not too busy. I recently did the 'Round the Island' ride to raise money for cancer. I'm a member of the local scout group and we did it together. It's about 60 miles. There are a lot of places here I still haven't seen, little villages you just don't get to.

I have a friend who lives on the eastern part of the Island and we make jokes about how it's almost like going to a foreign place when we meet because if you're going by public transport, you have to make so many arrangements.

Rachel: A lot of people think we're hill-billies out here. They ask me where I live and I say Ningwood, and they don't know it, so I say Shalfleet, but some don't know that either, so I say Yarmouth. Matthew and I have lived here all our lives so we don't know what it's like to be in a town, but we don't have any regrets.

Matthew: We have a little sailing boat in Newtown Creek, which is about a mile and a half away, and it's such a nice area to sail in. We hope to race it at some stage.

Rachel: I don't have much to do with the farm except for the calves. When I was 7, Dad said I should come and see a new heifer calf. He took me up to the farm, brought out a new rope halter, put it on the calf, and said why didn't I have a go at walking her? When they're young, they're so sweet and I instantly fell in love with the idea of walking them around. I took them to my first show that year. I was 8 and in the under-11 class for junior handlers. But when it came to it I was in tears because I didn't want to go into the ring. It was so daunting, with all those men showing cattle. But the next year I did the County Show and Craft Show, and we now go further afield to the All Britain Calf Show.

The day before a show, I get up about 6 o'clock, put on my overalls, go up to the farm, sometimes when it's still dark, get the calves on the halters, tie them up and finish off any clipping that needs doing. At 7 o'clock Matthew might come and join us, and we walk the calves round the yard for a while, getting them used to the idea of being in a ring. Then we brush and wash them, which is a messy job and you get absolutely drenched, but it's nice on a hot day and I think they enjoy it too.

Some of them can be really wild at the beginning, so you go up to them and stroke them a bit, and talk to them, then slip the halter over their heads which they absolutely hate. But you feed them small titbits and brush them and let them know you're not a big bully and not going to hurt them.

The judges look for your presentation and you have to try and cover any faults the calf might have. I get nervous at the major shows. There are people from all over Britain. Two years ago I won my class at the National Holstein Show, and I've also come seventh at the All Britain Holstein Calf Show.

I do like being involved with the animals. I can walk in the field here and it's a lovely feeling to think that some of them know you. Recently we sold one of my ex-show calves. I took her into the sale ring and someone bought her, and I thought, 'Oh no'. I don't enjoy the tractors or machinery side of farming. At the moment my main ambition is to be a large-animal vet.

Another thing I like doing is playing the trombone. There's a lot of music for young people on the Island. If you have music lessons at school and get to a certain level, the teacher says she'd like to see you at the Music Centre in Newport on Saturday mornings. There must be about 500 youngsters there who come for two and a half hours every week. There's a county youth orchestra, county youth wind band, jazz and string orchestras, keyboard workshops. It used to be free but they've just started charging for it, and they run a bus service for people to get to the Centre from all over the Island. In June (1995) I was accepted for the county youth orchestra.

I don't get out much with my friends. Saturday is the only free time I have and then I'm at the Music Centre. Sometimes we go to the cinema, Mum takes me, and I stay at a friend's house. I don't venture to the other side of the Island as much as Matthew does.

There isn't a university here, but there is the Isle of Wight College at Newport, though it only has a limited number of courses. Most people want to go away. It's such a small place, and there aren't many opportunities. So many people are getting 'A' grades now, the competition is that much stronger.

Matthew: I'm quite interested in law and am hoping to visit a magistrate's court in Portsmouth. I'd like to go away from the Island and then come back later on. A lot of the time you forget it is an island, but when you're on top of a bus and can see the sea, you realize what a lovely place it is.

Rachel: Ideally I think we should have a fixed link with the mainland just for Islanders, and no one else should use it! At present, there are reduced prices on ferries until you're 16, but on the buses it's only to 14, and then you pay adult prices. In summer we can't go direct to Newport by bus from here, because the bus company runs the Island Explorer which takes tourists by a scenic route, and you have to pay for that, though I think you can go direct at certain times. But the regular bus service, which isn't that regular from here, goes all round the houses.

The Musician and Publican

Cephas Howard, 60, comes from Cheshire. He studied design at the Regional College in Manchester and the Royal College of Art in London, where the Temperance Seven began playing together. He worked as a designer for the BBC's Light Entertainment Department, playing trumpet with the Temperance Seven in the evenings. In 1972 the band performed on Shanklin pier and he liked the Isle of Wight so much, he and his wife Jan decided to live here. They bought a pottery on Shanklin Esplanade before moving to Arreton where they opened a craft centre, a bistro and a pub. They have three children, and Cephas has a son by a previous marriage.

This was a derelict farm when we first came and what's now the bistro was full of cow manure. We did most of the building work ourselves – I'm an avid collector of architectural rubbish. The craftsmen we have here are a blacksmith, woodworker, potter, and my wife Jan has a shop. We print our own fabrics and plan to go into manufacturing cushions, bed throws and aprons.

That strip of water (the Solent) is the worst thing about the Isle of Wight because it prevents people coming here for an evening meal. We have a good ambience, good food, we're half an hour from Portsmouth and there's nothing to stop them getting on a boat and coming, except the cost of the water. So they don't come. Young people who are striving to make the Island a thriving place are being thwarted by those who have retired here and don't want anything to change.

The Temperance Seven still come to the Island sometimes, and we have some jolly good local musicians – jazz, rap, blues and classical. The leader of the London Symphony Orchestra lives on the Island. Many of the schools have really good bands and I've got two here now whom I've employed since they were at school. In the evenings it's all candlelit and the log fire's going. We have a few sing-songs. There are no fruit or cigarette machines, no juke box, or carpet on the floor. It's just an old-fashioned pub which is getting rarer by the day. It's an enjoyable life and when we stop enjoying it, we'll stop doing it.

The Geologist

You can have big arguments about when the Isle of Wight separated from the mainland, but the most reasonable suggestion would be that it became an island about 8,000 years ago. Some 120 million years ago this area was a swampy river where dinosaurs roamed, got buried and became fossilized, which is why so many are found here today. But to a geologist, of course, dinosaurs are quite a minor and to some, irrelevant part of geology, and you can do much more interesting things, like walking through Sandown Bay and, with a little knowledge, unravel its history of 40 or 50 million years in terms of climate, geography, and what was living there.

The geology museum on the Island is very small but, because of the dinosaurs found here, I think we should have a purpose-built one of international standard. But the Island is a very strange place. People have this limited vision and I'd like to drag some of them screaming and yelling to the American museums I've seen and show them what can be done. A building doesn't have to be a blot on the landscape – it can be designed very sympathetically and the spin-off in terms of visitors would be tremendous.

My expertise is in the area of fossil mammals and they hardly see the light of day here, though the Island is brilliant for them. Shrews, the earliest mole in the world, come from the Isle of Wight, and I don't know anywhere else in Britain where I could guarantee to take people out in the field and find a fossil mammal's tooth. And I don't know anywhere else in Europe like Alum Bay, which must be the most well-known geological site in Britain. They say there are about twenty-four different hues of sand there, from white to deep red, in different layers within the rock. If you stand back and look, you can see bands of colour and, between them, fairly drab clays. What I would like to see here is a place devoted to the geology of the site. There's nothing to explain why the coloured sand is here. In fact, it's mainly due to iron staining of some sort.

One of the important things on the Island at present in geological terms is the subsidence under houses: they are being threatened in the Undercliff and geologists are trying to unravel what's going on there. We have a much greater variety of different rock types in a very small space compared to many parts of the world I've visited.

They say you know you're a geologist when you go and see a John Wayne movie, ignore the action in the foreground and look at the rocks behind. Once, when my kids were watching a cowboy film supposedly set in Wyoming, I said, 'That's not Wyoming, that's Utah'. 'How do you know, Dad?' they asked. I said, 'Because that Navajo sandstone is only found in certain areas and Wyoming's not one of them.'

Allan Insole, 53, was born in London. When he left school he studied pharmacy, and took a degree and Ph.D in geology at Bristol University. He was assistant curator in the geology department of Bristol City Museum until he came to the Isle of Wight in 1975 to become County Museum Officer. He is now a lecturer in adult education, a tour guide in the States, Chairman of the Island's Geological Society and Industrial Archaeology group, and President Elect of the Natural History and Archaeology Society. He is also Mayor of Sandown and a primary school governor. He has written *Discovering Fossils* and is co-author, with David Burdett, of *Discovering an Island*. He is married to Sarah Phillips, who has also been mayor of the town, and they have two sons and one daughter.

The Fossil Collector

Martin Simpson, 36, was born in Liverpool, studied geology at Glasgow University, and came to the Isle of Wight in 1979. He has written *Fossil Hunting on Dinosaur Island*, has a fossil shop at Blackgang Chine, and gives talks to schoolchildren.

When I was 20 I set myself a target of fifteen years to collect as many fossils as I could, and then I hit on the idea of taking people on beach trips to find their own. You get the south-westerly gales coming in in the winter and they batter the cliffs down, and the sea washes the bits out of the mud. The trick is knowing the local beaches, and what's in the different layers.

Dinosaurs are what everyone wants to collect and last year a lady walking her dog found a dinosaur's spine and brought it to me in the shop. 'We went back to the beach and it took three days to find the rest of it in the mud, but I eventually dug it all out except for the head. It's the most complete one I've got.

I try and get visiting schoolchildren interested, and they all go back home with something they've discovered for themselves. I tell them, 'This is 189 million years old. Put it in your hand and touch it.'

Collecting fossils does no harm to the environment – you can preserve them by collecting them.

The Seaview Hotelier

Seaview Hotel was built about 1820, and added to around 1900. The other day we found an old 'For Sale' poster from that period, boasting of stables for five or six horses. It has

1906 on the front of the building, but that's when a façade was put on.

When my parents, grandparents and great-grandparents came for their holidays, a steamer came into Seaview. It was called the *Sixpenny Sick* and I think it came from Southsea. At one time, there were thousands of day trippers.

A lot of actors and broadcasters come to our hotel: Richard Attenborough, Richard Todd, Alec Guinness, Cliff Michelmore have all been here. Politicians too: Virginia Bottomley, Norman Fowler and Peter Jay have houses here. I think there *is* something special about the place. People can enjoy themselves without the trappings of the twentieth century. There are no amusement arcades or video machines, you have to make your own entertainment. Children are safe, they can play where they want, have crab races on the beach and go around in groups of an evening.

In the third week of August there's an annual regatta and the rowing races are in skiffs which are about 40 years old and quite heavy because they're clinker built. In the 1920s there was a chap called Wells who used to sail here a lot and one day he decided he'd like to design a dinghy everyone could sail. He sketched a boat on the back of a cigarette packet, and got Fenton's in Portsmouth to build it. This was the first Seaview One Design and cost £70 to £80; today it would be up to about £7,000. I used to own one built in 1936, and now have one made in '62. Almost all the boats, about 170 of them, have been built by the Warren family here in Seaview. They have different coloured sails and when there's a fleet out there, it's quite a sight.

I quite envy people coming down here in the summer. They can relax and enjoy themselves and there's always lots of parties going on. In Cowes Week you get people going around in white ties, tails and mess jackets, and others in shirts and shorts, but they all join in together. I suppose you could say Seaview is the Fulham to Bembridge's Chelsea. Bembridge has a lot of lords and ladies, Seaview tends to have the knights.

Nick Hayward, 45, studied at a hotel school and worked in France, London and Cambridge before coming to the Isle of Wight in 1979 to run the Seaview Hotel in Seaview. His family have spent holidays here since the turn of the century and his grandparents used to drive along the shore in a horse-drawn carriage. The hotel has won the Restaurant of the Year award from Les Routiers, two red rosettes from the AA, and has been voted the Best Seaside Hotel of the Year by the *Good Hotel Guide*. He is married to Nicola, who is involved in the hotel's advertising and decorating programmes, and they have three children.

The Manager at Farringford

Anne Cerise, 42, comes from Cornwall. She took a three year course in hotel and catering administration at South Devon Technical College, and worked in hotels in London, Looe and Exeter before, fifteen years ago, becoming joint manager, with her husband, of Farringford Hotel, the house where Tennyson lived and worked. They have one son.

Farringford was the private home of the Tennyson family up to the Second World War, and it wasn't requisitioned for use during the war because of its national importance. A butler and housekeeper lived in the lodge across the road and looked after everything. In 1947 it was bought by Thomas Cook, but as it had only fifteen rooms and they couldn't get permission to add on to the bedrooms, they built cottages at the back. Sir Fred Pontin bought the hotel in 1963, and converted the cottages to self-catering units. A lot of the furniture in the library is original, including the chairs and big table where Tennyson wrote. Over the fireplace the names of Tennyson and his wife, Emily, are carved in the wood.

Many famous visitors came to Farringford at that time: Dickens, Lewis Carroll, Sir Arthur Sullivan, Charles Kingsley, Edward Lear, Jenny Lynd the singer (we still have her piano), Swinburne and Garibaldi, who planted a Wellingtonia (fir) in front of the house. It grew very big but died in 1980 as a result of the 1976 drought.

The present Lord Tennyson lives in South Africa; he's a great-great-nephew of the poet. I met the previous Lord Tennyson as well. He was a bachelor and remembered a lot about the house from Tennyson's time. The local Tennyson Society meet here in winter, the Tennyson Society from Lincoln have lectures in the library, and school groups come when they're studying Tennyson. A couple of our hotel guests have felt they couldn't sleep in Tennyson's bedroom itself. The atmosphere was too strong. It still has his huge wardrobes and chests of drawers.

Tennyson was a sociable person but he would pick and choose who he wanted to see. In fact, he had a spiral staircase escape route built from his library down to the conservatory. If someone he didn't like came in, he'd nip down that, and out to a summerhouse in the copse. That isn't there any more, and we don't use the spiral staircase because it's a bit wobbly.

The Walkers

Norman: When we were both 35 and I was working in the car industry, I used to go out in the morning when the kids were in bed and come back when they were back in bed,

Norman and Beryl Birch, both 52, come from St Helen's, near Liverpool. Norman worked in the car industry, and Beryl was a nursery nurse before they came to the Isle of Wight in 1979 to open a guest house. They have been married for thirty-two years and have a grown-up son and daughter. They now run the Hambledon Hotel in Shanklin and operate Step by Step Walking Holidays in the Isle of Wight.

and I began to think to myself, was this really what life was all about? We decided to change our way of life completely.

Beryl: We used to do a lot of walking up north and when we came here we got friendly with a couple who liked it too. We decided Sunday would be a hotel-banned day, and used to go off with this family for picnics and walks. Then Norman met someone in Isle of Wight tourism who thought we could organize a two-centre walking holiday.

Norman: Every now and then we got people asking about guided walks and we thought these would fill an odd weekend, but the project just mushroomed. By the time it comes to the end of this month (June 1995) I will have walked just over 9,000 miles since 1986 when we started which includes twelve times round the Island in the last eighteen months.

A lot of people think the Isle of Wight is just a place for bucket and spade holidays. But it's more than that. There are 513 miles of footpaths, more footpaths than actual roads, and over 2,300 signposts. I couldn't count the number of times people have said, 'I never realized the Isle of Wight was like this'. There are so many hundreds of acres that have been designated as areas of outstanding natural beauty with lovely downlands and many wooded walks. If I can show people these things, they start seeing the real true Isle of Wight and the beauty that's here. I think the Island's motto, 'All this beauty is of God', is one of the truest things ever said.

Beryl: It's a much milder climate here than on the mainland. People are amazed how forward nature is.

Norman: I don't aim my walking holidays at people who want to stroll for 2 or 3 miles. We average about 9 to 12 miles a day and have a pick-up lunch time service for those who don't want to walk any further.

I tell people all about the history of the place, who's lived here, just a general smattering. Most have come to walk, not have a history lesson. You can say, 'Well, Charles I was here in 1647 and was kept in Carisbrooke Castle and was then sent off to London and beheaded'. That's about as much as most people really want to know.

Maurice Lickens, 74, first came to the Isle of Wight during the war when in 1944 he was involved in the PLUTO (Pipe Line Under The Ocean) project. As a boy, he was the first from his school to represent England in soccer; he joined the Middlesex Yeomanry at 17, pretending he was 19 and forging his mother's signature on a parental consent form. He is an insurance broker, a member of Lloyd's, a Lord's Taverner and with his wife, **Barbara**, runs the Savoy Country Club near Yarmouth, which they bought in 1967 after having spent many holidays there. They have three children and seven grandchildren. In 1987 they hosted the international Special Olympics for mentally handicapped people.

The 'Special Games' Family

Maurice: When I heard the holiday camp was up for sale, I said to Barbara, 'What about buying it?' She said, 'Are you mad or drunk?' I really had no more intention of buying a holiday camp than flying, but we did. We were living in London then and always thought I'd semi-retire early, and that a little place like this would keep me out of mischief. In fact, it took over both our lives. We can now take just over 300 guests, and 200 in our self-catering bungalows. We have a leisure centre and sports hall and this is one of the few places in the south that can host international standard events for trampoline, badminton and snooker.

One day a fellow Lord's Taverner, Reg Campbell, rang me up and said they had nowhere to hold the 1987 Special Olympics and could we help? I said, 'Are you serious, how many people are you talking about?' He said we might get 700 to 800 contestants and it could cost £100,000. We set off to see Morris Barton, the leader of the County Council, and asked him what they could do for us. Not a lot, he said. I think he promised us £15,000. We rang a few like-minded friends who we thought might be daft enough to join us, and a few did. So we set about this monumental task which was to put on the games for however many mentally handicapped people wanted to compete. We had no venue, no money, no track, nothing.

But . . . we told the Special Olympics fraternity we would be running the games, got literature prepared, entry forms sent out, and decided which sports to include. Medina School said they'd got a grass track and we found we could hire a grandstand from the Council, who raised their £15,000 grant to £20,000 to cover its cost.

We were waiting for entrants to come in at that time, and the numbers got to 700, then 1,000, then 1,200, including contestants from nine overseas countries. This is the largest number that has ever participated in the Special Olympics right up to today.

In fact, the games turned out to be the greatest unifying thing that has ever happened on the Isle of Wight. Bob Foxall agreed to be the administrator, Peter Taylor the treasurer, and we got old people, kids' clubs, and pubs all over the Island to help. People who at the beginning hadn't wanted to be associated with it, suddenly started ringing in asking to be involved. The Duchess of Gloucester came to open it, and it was a wonderful event.

In the end, we had money left over and the Charity Commission said we could use it for other purposes as long as they were for mentally handicapped people and connected with sport. I'd just spent nearly £1 million building a sports and leisure complex and we thought no one in the world was doing indoor games for mentally handicapped people, so why didn't we? Since then, we've had an annual six-day Indoor Games event with snooker, weight lifting, cricket, darts. Our top number of entrants has been 650, with ages from 12 upwards, and they come from all over the UK and abroad.

The closing ceremony is a real tear-jerker – I think you have to experience it to understand. A band marches in, then the competitors sporting their medals. Last year Ryde School choir sang, there were trampoline and dancing displays. Being the chairman, I thank those who made it possible, but I have difficulty not going overboard because not enough do enough for this kind of person. When locals come for the opening ceremony, they love it, but again not as many come as I would like, though I think the number is growing. The closing ceremony, as far as I'm concerned, justifies this bloody idiot spending the best part of £1 million to build this sports hall even if it was never used for anything else.

Barbara: To see those kids on that last night and their total joy, waving and coming to shake hands with you, is quite something. In general, a lot is done to try and segregate mentally handicapped people, but if you see them together, it's wonderful because they have such a good time on their own level. I think there's an awful lot to be said for letting them socialize with each other.

Another thing we do have here is holidays for mentally and physically handicapped people, and for eight weeks every year we give the place over to them, though other guests can come if they want to. Some local councils have been sending people for twenty-five years now – we've had 30,000 from Sandwell (West Bromwich). There's lots of things for them to do, like swimming lessons every day if they want them, and we have a special chair in the pool paid for by other guests. We have lots of fund-raising events during the year.

Maurice: I think the games don't get enough publicity. We can't do it because we don't want people to say aren't we good? We hold them here because we want to. And because competitors enjoy them. They always call me Mr L. and I was going through Cowes the other day when one young man who'd taken part in one of the Indoor Games events, called out from across the street, 'Mr L., Mr L., I've been practising. I'm going to win that bloody weights this year'.

The Holiday Park Family

My father was one of nine and virtually all the family except one aunt worked here at one time. Father is now 86 and still gets here every morning before everyone else, spotting things that need doing. He was originally a boatbuilder but after the war he made two caravans. His brothers owned some land, and between them they set up the holiday camp business.

We now have 221 chalets, which we own, about 40 caravans, some privately owned, and 450-odd camping pitches for caravans and tents. We can take about 2,200 people in the high season. There's a club, bar, entertainment, discotheque, an indoor swimming pool, children's pool, sauna, jacuzzi. . . . We also have B & B accommodation, self-catering, and restaurants for people who don't want to cook. There are about ninety staff in the high season, and twenty-nine employed all the year round.

We own 400 ft of beach, but this doesn't have the draw it used to. People go out and about to where they can get the car, they don't seem to want to walk any more. The beach might not be as popular as it was, but you get down there at seven or eight in the morning and it really is beautiful. The sun's there, it's just . . . peaceful. And that's what people find. The Isle of Wight pace of life is just that little bit slower.

We're still a private family business and can't afford the marketing expenses of those in the big boys' league. Hopefully we can trade on our customer service. We still have clients who remember me carrying their luggage in my school holidays. I used to stand by the bus stop with a cart and take it up for them.

Years ago we had about 60 per cent repeat business. Now it's down to 50 per cent. After the war, people were so regimented, they'd find a place they liked to go on holiday and go back year in, year out. Last week we had a chap here who was my age – I used to play with him when I was a nipper. His father comes here for old time's sake, but he will go abroad, and come back to us every two or three years.

The most important thing for the Isle of Wight is for those of us in the tourist trade to try and work more closely together. We do so more than we used to, but I still think there could be tighter co-operation. Maybe we will be able to do this through the new Tourism Partnership that's been set up. I'd hate to see us going back to the bad old days when everyone was very protective of their own style of holiday or town. We were at a Birmingham exhibition recently selling camping/touring holidays, and someone came up and said, 'You can't get touring caravans on the Isle of Wight'. He didn't know you could. This shows how we get mixed in with islands like Jersey, where you can't take them.

The Isle of Wight is a nice place to come to. The disadvantage is the cost of the ferry. I have mixed views on a tunnel or bridge to the mainland. Overall I don't like the

Martin Humphray, 50, left school at 15, went to the local technical college and began work as an electrician in Whitecliff Bay Holiday Park, Bembridge, which was started by his father and two uncles in 1949 and is still a family business. He has been a parish councillor, Chairman of the local Camera Club, and played darts for London. He is now the managing director of the 45 acre holiday park. He is married to Stephanie, the assistant catering manageress, and they have a 16-year-old daughter. His sister, Gerry, is joint manageress of the shop; his cousin John is a director of the company.

David Wood, 47, comes from Essex. At 15 he went to America to help his father train chimpanzees for PG Tips advertisements. He worked in America and Australia as a comedian and singer before coming back to Britain and training as a chef. He joined the RAF at 20, and became a radar operator on Nimrod anti-submarine warfare aircraft. From 1979 to 1982 he was on Vulcan V Bombers (serving in the Falklands War) and was captain of a Nimrod. He went to Cyprus as Deputy Senior Officer Controller and was a Flight Commander at the RAF college at Cranwell when the Gulf War started. He was involved in supporting Special Operations and later in Operation Provide Comfort, giving help to Kurds and Marsh Arabs. He opened Seaward Guest House in Ryde in 1992, and is Executive Secretary of the All Island Tourist Industry Association and Chairman of its Medina Branch. He has been married twice and has one daughter.

idea but there are times when I'd like to go to the mainland and can't. The subject needs a great deal of sensible not political research. There are other areas where they've linked islands and it hasn't spoiled them, so why should it spoil the Isle of Wight?

The Guest House Owner

Why did I open a guest house? I wanted to calm down and I liked the Isle of Wight and the life here. When Dad died and left me some money, I decided to come and live here. It costs a little more than being in Surbiton but it's much nicer than Surbiton. And I've lived there as well!

The good thing about the Island is that you can get a boat from the mainland and feel that you're going somewhere different, rather than just driving down a road or getting into a train. And it is different. But we must encourage more overseas visitors to come, and advertise the places we have that will attract them. Foreign visitors last year spent £9 million. Domestic visitors spent £222 million. Foreign visitors to Berkshire spent £236 million. What's in Berkshire that attracts people? Windsor Castle. On the Isle of Wight we have Carisbrooke Castle, where the last king of England to be executed spent his last days; and Osborne House, the home of Queen Victoria. But these are not being marketed properly because they belong to bigger organizations like English Heritage and National Trust who advertise their properties as a whole.

Two years ago, Mel Williams, then of Wightlink, had the idea of starting an Image Campaign to make people aware of the Island and how many things there are to do here. We found in the north of England only something like two out of ten knew where it was. In the Midlands, it was about two and a half to three out of ten. The Image Campaign is a five year project and we're now advertising in newspapers and the London Underground. I've been pushing for TV advertising because that's the greatest force, and this year we've gone for that too, and it seems to be having an effect.

I think there is always a market on the Isle of Wight for moderately priced accommodation. The majority of people I get staying here are family groups with two or three children. They want bed, breakfast and an evening meal, and to know what they're paying for before they start. It's the lower income bracket who are coming here. I don't care what anyone says, you are never going to attract people with vast amounts of disposable income any more. They might come for a short break or long week-end, but not a long holiday.

A magazine recently called the Island 'a diamond in the Atlantic'. Not quite accurate, but it is diamond-shaped. It's a lovely green island with sandy beaches, rolling downs, rugged coastline, all in a very compact place. Quite a lot of my visitors book for a week and find it's not long enough, there's too much to do. I've made a point of going round all the attractions and only been disappointed in two or three.

The Director of Tourism

Islands are in my blood so I found it fairly easy to understand some of the problems and aspirations people have here. I think islanders always tend to look at themselves and not take a broader perspective. There's a feeling they're not part of the mainland and there is a sense of isolation.

I think the Isle of Wight has tremendous potential. What struck me when I first came was that it has so many 'attractions' and I do feel the Island has been hidden. But people here have made tremendous efforts over the last two years to overcome this lack of visibility, though you talk to those who come on business or for a holiday, and they're still amazed at what it has to offer: good beaches, lovely countryside, pretty villages and well over a hundred places of interest, from big ones like Blackgang Chine to smaller ones like Molly Attrill's pottery.

We now have 2.4 million visitors a year, of which 1 million are day visitors. Roughly 30 per cent stay for a short break (three nights or less) and just over 30 per cent come out of season between October and March. About 26 per cent of the population are employed in tourism and it generates roughly £200 million a year into the Island's economy.

Geoff Le Page, 47, was born and brought up in Guernsey. At 18 he went on a marketing and administration training course with British European Airways in London and stayed for fifteen years. He worked for ten years with Horizon Holidays in Birmingham before coming to the Isle of Wight in 1993 as Director of Tourism. He is married to Jenny and they have three children.

Isle of Wight Tourism has an overall budget of about £1.8 million. It's adequate, but when you compare that to our competitors, Guernsey or Jersey who have budgets of £5 or £6 million, it doesn't leave a lot to promote the Island, although all our publications are paid for by advertising.

I think our Image Campaign (see page 120) has changed the profile of the Island. It started when the tourism industry saw there was a need to do something. Visitor numbers had been declining for several years and this had to be reversed. The Campaign has had a great effect in the two years we've run it, with the national press, advertisements in the London Underground and on television. We're all working together to promote the Island as a whole, rather than individual places like say, Sandown or Shanklin. These towns *are* competitors, but we can't afford to promote each of them separately. And if visitors come to the Island, everyone will benefit. It's what I call synergistic marketing, two and two make five. If we all pull together, we'll get more out of it.

Certainly, more visitors are coming outside the main traditional holiday season than they were twenty years ago. There is a feeling we have a lot of old people here and in some months of the year we do, but in other months you'll see school parties, and our main and most successful market is the traditional family holiday. And, of course, we have a whole range of big events like Cowes Week, the classic boat and power boat festivals, and the European windsurfing championships at Sandown.

The majority of our beaches have Tidy Britain awards, but we don't have any European Blue Flags. There has been steady improvement in the quality of sea water, though undoubtedly some people would say it hasn't gone far or fast enough. The water is clean and safe but we're in the English Channel and there are always going to be problems when things are washed overboard from ships. There are notices up which tell you about the quality of the water – samples are taken weekly – and people can decide for themselves whether to go in. But in my view, water testing processes are not all they lead us to believe. You can test one part of the water on a beach and that 1 per cent may have a problem, but there could be no problem in the rest of it.

What I would most like to do is to continue improving the image of the Island, and make tourism an all year round business. That would reduce seasonal unemployment and, of course, bring more money into the economy.

The Press and PR Manager

The main thing I do is promote the Island through journalism, television, radio and film work. I invite journalists to the Island to write about it, do editorial features myself for magazines, meet directors and producers in London and say what a wonderful product we have down here.

For the last two years, we've had more money to spend on press and publicity because of the Image Campaign. This was started when cross-Solent operators and the Council got together with hoteliers and places of interest owners, to put money – half a million pounds each year so far – towards promoting the Island. In a normal year, my budget for Isle of Wight Tourism is very small but with the Image Campaign we've been able to spend more.

We've just finished working with Fiji television who are making twenty-six five minute programmes about B & B places on the Island linked with places of interest. We've had Hong Kong television over here recently, and quite a lot of German and Dutch journalists. I think in August (1995) we had about thirteen film crews from the BBC, London Week-end, Granada, as well as foreign crews. Ken Russell filmed part of *Lady Chatterley* here, Jasper Carrott and Robert Powell filmed here, and Michael Palin made four half-hour TV programmes.

We've filmed embryo transplants for rare breeds, tomatoes in glasshouses pollinated by Dutch bumblebees. I recently took a Japanese film crew to Little Upton Farm. They had gone down the garden and the farmer said to me he'd have to go as he'd got a cow in calf. I went with him into the shed and the next minute I was standing up to my knees in hay, sleeves rolled up, hanging on to a piece of rope attached to the calf's hooves, trying to winch it out. The crew arrived just in time to film the birth and they gave it (the film) to the farmer so he could use it for school visits.

Jane Jones, 50, was born in Slough. She worked as an Army nurse in the Queen Alexandra's Royal Army Nursing Corps, got married, and when she and her husband were not allowed to work in the same Army unit, she began writing for British Forces broadcasting units and British newspapers. She has since worked in Cyprus, Aberdeen, the Middle East, Hong Kong and for Grampian television. Eleven years ago she returned to the Isle of Wight, where her grandmother and parents had lived, and which she'd visited as a child; six years ago she became Press and Public Relations Manager for Isle of Wight Tourism. She is divorced and has two children and four grandsons.

I've met some wonderful characters on the Island that I might not have known about otherwise. One day with a location manager I banged on a front door, and you could hear the sound echoing all through the house. Then we heard this shuffling and an old gentleman opened the door. He must have been about 80 and had a white pinny on. I said we were from television, and he said, 'Hang on a minute, I'll go and get the mistress'. Then this old lady in a grey twin-set and pearls and white lace gloves came out. She must have been about 94. I think he'd been working for her for forty years, and they invited us in for tea.

It seems once people come here, they return many times. A lot of hoteliers who've been in the business for forty-odd years, still have people visiting who came the first week they opened. A bit like me. I've been coming here all my life. I have photographs of myself in the paddling pool at Ventnor when I was 3, by the donkey wheel at Carisbrooke Castle at 7. These days I enjoy going to London and the buzz of a faster pace of life, but I miss the Island if I'm away for more than a week, and I love coming back.

Glen London, 36, comes from Sydney, Australia, and met his English wife, Sarah, out there. Her family comes from the Isle of Wight and five years ago Glen and Sarah came to work in the UK. He has been in radio in Australia and London and three years ago came to work with Isle of Wight Radio, first as sales manager and sales director and now station manager.

The Radio Station Manager

The Isle of Wight has one of the smallest radio stations in the UK and we don't have an engineer on the Island. But one does come over on Saturdays for maintenance and when something goes wrong we have a back-up system – a tape of songs we've pre-recorded. If everything fails, there's another station we can relay over.

We have eight full-time staff and a number of freelances, and I think we run this station at the level of any mainland one. We do our own road shows, give away prizes, have games and music, and local news on the hour every hour.

Probably the bulk of our audience is aged between 25 and 54 years old, slightly female biased. On the advertising side, we do very well with anything to do with the home. We wouldn't do well with 16 to 20 year olds. They listen to Power FM. We're on air sixteen hours a day, 6 a.m. to 10 p.m., then we take an overnight service.

I've worked in six radio stations and I've never heard listeners being so vocal in their criticisms as they are here.

Although this is a negative thing, they must be listening to criticize. They say why don't we play jazz, country and western, classical, music from the '40s and '50s, black dance music? But we can't play them all, we have to stick to a format and a lot of people don't understand that. They seem quite amiable when we contact them, and say they do like the station but, for instance, they don't like the way we pronounce certain words. It's better to have criticism than silence.

Maybe people would like more local news, more gossipy-type stuff. But we are primarily a music format station with a certain amount of speech content, and I believe the vast majority only want a couple of minutes of speech and then you've got to get out of it. We find a lot of under 50 year olds won't persevere with ten or fifteen minutes of chat. They're more likely to change programmes. The 55+ listeners are what we call the BBC audience. They've been brought up on it and it's slower, more laborious. The new commercial radio users want something snappy, segmented. So after two or three minutes of talk, they'll say that's very interesting, now let's get to the bottom line and have another record.

The Radio Reporter

My name goes back to Roman times and I'm very proud to be an Islander. If I spend a day on the mainland, I'm always glad to come back on the ferry in the evening. When I was at college in Portsmouth I had to get up at 6 o'clock in the morning to catch the 7.30 catamaran to the mainland, which for a young student was quite hard work. I had the option of moving into digs on the mainland, but wanted to come back here every day even though it did cost a lot of money. It wasn't only me, quite a lot of students did that too.

It's very laid back here; you don't have fast cars and motorways. I think if I was from the mainland and used to a quicker pace, I'd soon get fed up and want to go back, but if you're born here, it's an environment you don't want to leave. It's strange having this uniqueness, yet being so near to the mainland. But it does depend on the person, of course. My sister was born and bred here and she's at

Justin Gladdis, 23, was born and brought up on the Isle of Wight, went to college in Portsmouth, and now works as a radio reporter with Isle of Wight Radio.

university in London and has no desire to come back, and a lot of my old school friends have now moved away, too.

I think I'm suited to working in radio here – I know what the Island's all about. I select the news I read, and report on the stories I think will be interesting to Islanders.

The Boatbuilder

Michael Stewart Warren, 47, was born on the Island, and is the third generation of his family to live and work in Seaview. His grandfather, a boatbuilder (as was his father), had come from Gosport in 1936. He did his apprenticeship with another company before joining his father in the family business. He is married to Monica and they have three children.

We've always specialized in making the Seaview One Design dinghies and they're only built in Seaview. They are clinker boats (the planks are lapped on top of each other) designed for one person to race in, though you can get four in if you just want to cruise around. We started building them in the thirties and now there's a fleet of about 170 here in the village.

A lot of boatbuilding firms went out of business when fibre glass came in, but instead of trying to keep going, we concentrated on the maintenance and mooring side of the business until wooden boats came into their own again. Over the last twelve years we've had a boom in building them, despite the recession. It seems to go in phases. My father built about thirty in a row, then slowed back down. Now, twenty-five years down the line, we've had a run of sixty on the run, and I think we'll slow down a bit now. My father built fifty-two of them, I've built seventy so far, and we've got orders for three more. New people come into the village, and the yacht club provides more training for the younger ones.

We can never compete in price with fibre glass – it takes one person about nine weeks to build a Seaview dinghy and you never build two exactly the same. But I can look at most of those I've built and, even from a distance, can normally tell which boat it is. I don't need to look at names, I just look at the grain on the timber and the name will come to mind. I don't think we've lost a boat since the '50s when one was washed off the slipway.

The boats cost about £7,000 and we provide a full package: we make them, do the maintenance, fit them out, put on the sails, put them afloat and do the moorings. In September we bring them in, de-rig them, wash them out and put them in store. There are times at the beginning of the season when I have eight hands to help, in winter we drop down to three boatbuilders. I'm more into making the boats than the book side, which my wife does. My oldest son works for another firm and helps me out in the evenings.

The dinghies usually go out mid-July and finish one or two weeks after the August Bank Holiday, if we don't have bad weather. Families have individual colours for their sails, so you have a mass of colour out there when they're racing, sometimes fleets of up to 100 boats at a time. They're used by a great age range of people, from 12 year olds to those in their 70s, and are normally handed down in the same way Seaview houses are.

In winter, when it blows too hard, say about a force 6, we have to bring the dinghies ashore, and that takes us about six hours. In my father's time, he would line the seafront with them, and there wouldn't be a car in sight or any complaints. Now when I get the boats in, straightaway people will be moaning they can't park their cars outside their houses. It gives us major headaches because once we have them ashore, we have to start moving them or I have the police on my back. We store them all round the village – in an old chapel, sheds, garages, builders' yards, churches. We have a workshop in Rope Walk and that's where we hide ourselves in the winter months and just get on with building boats.

The Cornish Craftsman

The only reason I left Scilly was because Jennie was teaching on the mainland and couldn't get a job in Scilly. I was a stonemason. Well, it was a trade I practised more than anything else. There were a couple of brilliant characters who'd taught me everything I knew. Then I worked for myself doing general building on the islands of Bryher and Tresco, rowing back and forth for fifteen years. Sometimes there was a bit of a hooley, believe you me.

The Isle of Wight is exactly the same as Scilly except on a bigger scale. There's no doubt about it, you do feel you're living on an island. There's talk about putting a bridge across here, some say it would be ideal and open up the

William (Bill) Pender, 50, stonemason, boatmaker and boat repairer, was born in the Isles of Scilly. He is married to Jennie and they have two children.

Island. But I'm one of those who believe the worst thing that ever happened to this country was building that bloody Channel tunnel. The worst thing that could happen to this Island would be to build a bridge or tunnel to the mainland. It would lose its identity. When an area gets popular, people want to go there and the indigenous people fizzle out. Then you've got a place where people go on holiday, partially to see the Island, partially to see the local people and in the end, there aren't any local people.

When I'm asked here if I'm local, I say, 'Yes, I'm an islander'. 'Haven't seen you before,' they say. 'I don't expect you have,' I say. 'I don't come from here, but I come from an island. I'm still an islander.' There's no doubt we're different from mainland people. You put ten islanders against ten mainlanders, and you'll find the island person will be able to turn his hands to most things because he's had to, he hasn't been able to run down to a shop or get someone else to do it for him.

By the time I've finished the housework, which is as boring as hell, I come down here to the shed, and I've always got something to do. In a fortnight this 30 ft rowing boat I've been repairing will be finished. I'm making a water wheel to go in my aviary which should keep going round without losing water. I wouldn't go so far as to say I'm an inventor. I see things fairly straightforward. I've been doing bits and pieces for a chap down the road. We started off with an empty house, now it's nearly complete.

There are three things I can't do: have a baby, the electrics, and paint. I hate painting. If I'm working for an old lady and she asked me to paint something, I'd do it, but if she had a husband capable of doing it, I'd say no. I like wood most. You can be very crude with it, and it will still do its job, or go over the top and it can really come to life. I find a lot of driftwood on the shore, a root or a tree that's been rolling around the beach, and I just put a coat of varnish on it, and it's a feature unto itself, quite beautiful really. Every time I go past a skip I take out bits of wood. I can't imagine why people throw them away.

One of these days, Kit, my son, and I are going to build ourselves a 20 ft rowing boat with four seats so we can have mixed crew for youngsters. It will be named properly with a bottle of Champagne over it. Boats are living things, you've got to put a lot of trust in them, so you've got to do them properly. If you treat them right, they treat you right.

We've done up three boats now for the same chappie. I don't charge, I do it for the fun and enjoyment, and he brings down several bottles of wine for people to consume at the launch. Nobody ever thinks of re-christening them, so each time I've taken my glass across and poured my drink over the boat and christened her again. Then I go back for another glassful!

The Chair Maker

It's funny how I got into chair making. It started as a hobby in 1987 after the storm. A lot of trees had blown down and we had a glut of timber about. I belonged to a boat club at the time and we used to burn all the wood, but I thought there must be a use for it. I've always had an interest in woodwork and began making a Windsor chair, which I'd read about in books. It has a solid seat, the legs socketed in to the bottom, and the spindles into the top.

I taught myself, learnt by my mistakes and went on from there. I use modern power tools as well as hand ones which are better for some jobs. I think if my forefathers had had electricity, they would have used that, too. The wood for the seat is ash, and that comes from the mainland, but the rest is made with local green wood which I split with the grain. It's a traditional method going back to the 1700s. I buy the wood from the contractors when they're clearing an area in the forest.

I split the logs to the size I want, shape them up, put them into a steam chest, which is basically a pipe with hot steam going into it, leave them there a couple of hours and then bend the wood round a 'former' (a mould). You can bend oak and beach, but ash is the best. You have about forty-five seconds once you've taken the split logs out of the steamer. You have to work quick, clap it on to the former, then bend it. You don't get a second chance. The greener the wood is the better, and if you can use a tree cut yesterday, all the sap's still there. If it's dry, to my wife's disgust, I soak it in our fish pond.

Paul Wise, 42, moved to the Isle of Wight from Surrey when he was 16. He became a motor mechanic apprentice, took an engineering course, and worked in Samuel White's shipyard before being made redundant in 1982. He was a self-employed gardener until 1991, since when he's been making chairs professionally. He lives in Whippingham and is married to Joyce.

About 80 per cent of my chair legs are made on the pole lathe when I'm showing at local events, like the Garlic Festival and the Forest Fair, and I give talks to local groups about chair bodging.

A bodger was a person who worked out in the forest, turning up chair legs all day and night and sleeping there in the summer. There's a theory the word comes from a German barrel maker called Bottcher, which is quite close to bodger, and I think he used similar tools. But you shouldn't confuse 'bodge' and 'botch'. I've been told that 'botch' may come from the Tay Bridge disaster when it was discovered that sub-standard materials had been used and the builder was called Mr Booch.

When I first started I had four chair designs, now I'm up to nine: rocking chairs, wheelback, double bow, hoop back, a continuous arm bow, carver. . . . Every winter I sit down and draw up plans from old photographs for another one. People don't usually look at a chair and think I've got to have a set, but sometimes they come back a couple of years later. I've been lucky really. I've normally not had less than a five to six month waiting list for my chairs since I started, and that's four years ago now.

The Flying Machine Man

I had visited the Island before and had a friend with a house in Cowes. When I told her of our project (to design a boat) she said, 'Right, come and stay with us, we'll find you a shed and you can start next week'. We moved in, built the boat and won the Weymouth Speed trials with it.

One night I was at a party and met someone who had been hang-gliding. By the end of the evening four of us had bought his glider for £25 each. In those days hang-gliding was literally ground-skimming down the hill, hopefully missing gorse bushes and barbed wire fences on the way. The heroes were those who actually managed to stay up for thirty seconds. I was designing boats but my thoughts were turning to making hang-gliders. When you're learning about something, you think other people are the experts, but then they give you clues that they haven't thought of

Rory Carter, 46, was born in America, studied civil engineering and yacht design in Southampton, worked for a boatbuilder in Kent, and came to the Isle of Wight to design a boat a friend was going to make. He is now Chairman of Airwave Gliders Ltd. He is married to Patsy and they have three sons.

everything, and perhaps there's an opening for someone to do something better.

So I designed and built a fairly radical hang-glider but my method of steering didn't work and after a few attempts I decided it was not a good idea to continue with it. A local chap told me the Americans had just come up with a fantastic new design, so I went to have a look at it with a New Zealander, a superb sailmaker, and in 1979 we started our company, Airwave, to build hang-gliders here and sell to Europe. We started in an old school, and in 1986 bought a place at Shalfleet. When we later got into paragliding and needed more space, we bought a big hangar in Cowes as well.

We went from strength to strength on the sail-making front, and peaked at about 1,000 hang-gliders a year in the mid-1980s. We set up a sister company in America and had good dealers in Germany, Japan, America and South Africa. Today, our sale of hang-gliders has diminished somewhat because paragliding has taken over. We're probably making 300 or 400 a year now, with prices from £2,000 to £3,000; and 1,500 to 2,000 paragliders, priced a little lower.

We have about forty people working here in the winter and sixty to seventy in the summer. In the mid-1980s, we took on the then world champion hang-gliding pilot, John Pendry, and he became our marketing man. Today we support a whole range of pilots. We're the only company making gliders on the Isle of Wight – there's only one other in the UK – and the only company making paragliders in the UK. All our ordinary materials, sail cloth, aluminium, nuts and bolts, come over on national carriers and they don't charge any more for bringing them across.

From the mid- to late 1980s, we won hang-gliding world championships, cross-country records, and European and various national titles. We're just getting to the point where our competition paragliders are up with the best, but it's taken six years to do this.

Although the standard of living here is lower, the quality of life is higher than on the mainland. And any disadvantages are small compared to the advantages: the countryside, the beaches, mountain biking up in the hills. I've got a 36 ft racing cruiser and have just won the single-handed Nab Tower race. I've also won the single-handed Round the Island Race several times. It's about 60 miles and usually takes about twelve hours.

And there's hang-gliding. It's Superman, cape flying behind him! It's that feeling of being able to fly close to the ground and just swoop and dive and be in control. You can fly above people on the ground and talk to them, then turn around and go up again. Flying cross-country is a great challenge. You take off on a day like yesterday when there were huge clouds going up everywhere, and very soon you hit this bumpy air which is a thermal, circle in it, and go up rapidly. It's like an elevator. You get into the smooth air between the clouds, go in a straight line, glide for the next piece of lift, decide whether you want to go up or down, and then go and look for the next thermal, which is generally by a cornfield or tarmac which heats up and creates a blob of unstable air, and suddenly you just go up like a huge mushroom. You sometimes see this rising air because it has birds in it, or straw and insects buzzing around. As you bump into it, you get the turbulence, circle in it, and up you go again. It's just a whole different world.

The Airfield Manager

The airport is farmland leased from John Taylor, and about 193 people work here now. Hangar 1 is where it all first started in the early '60s, and a lot of the original design work was done at the nearby Propeller Inn! I remember the early maiden flights of the different aircraft. All the families involved used to come and see them take off. Everyone would ask, 'Is it alright?' It was very exciting, and a new concept for the Isle of Wight, too. We hadn't had any planemakers here before that and many of the staff were taken from different jobs and trained to work on planes. We were all thrown together with a lot of enthusiasm and support from Desmond (Norman) and John (Britten). They really were the good old days.

Now we have something like 9,500 'movements' a year – with company test flights, pleasure flying, gliders. Nobody on the Island has any air transport but there is an air training school across the road where we familiarize pilots with our planes and give engineers an understanding of maintenance work.

The planes were originally built here, but in the last fifteen years, they've been produced in Romania under licence and then sent to us. We customize them, which could mean taking them to pieces and putting on the different modifications (radios and navigation aids). We've produced about 1,260 planes and sell to 112 countries. The planes are used for a variety of purposes: surveillance in fishery protected zones, fitted with skis at Mt Cook in New Zealand, for geological surveys, fire quenching and crop-spraying. . . .

The Islander has the longest production run of any British aircraft since the war. In fact it's one of the few still in production. It's a life-line to islanders round the world. I think the shortest route is in the Shetlands. It takes about five minutes, you get up to take-off speed, get elevated, and come down. When we do the repair work on these planes, we sometimes see sheep droppings inside – you can get four or five sheep in there for a few minutes.

We've just completed an order for six planes for Australia, the Cook Islands have some, and the Falklands. We ferry them all out ourselves. We did have difficulties during the Falklands War. The aircraft were test-flown here and completed, disassembled, and put in huge crates. These went by sea, and the two fitters went down by courtesy of the RAF to put them back together again.

Last year we had two developments. We 'stretched' one plane and introduced radar in the front bulbous nose, and made another – a twelve seater. There are always ideas for improvements and modifications but the development money just isn't there. I don't believe the government has ever supported this particular project. We've had to struggle over the years and I think there has always been an edge of disappointment from the beginning that they didn't back us, as we are one of the only proven aircraft manufacturers in the country. I suppose the fact they've purchased Islanders for the MOD in the last five or six years is something. There are eight planes flying with the Army now. We've had many ministerial visits but not seen any development money yet. When you have a design and someone says, 'Will it work?' I can understand the

Bruce Jacobs, 54, was born in Ventnor, the third generation of his family to be born on the Island. He was a joiner pattern maker in the building trade before coming to Britten-Norman Ltd in 1966. This was a company founded in the late 1950s by aeronautical engineers John Britten and Desmond Norman when they became aware of the need, through their international crop-spraying business, for a light twin-engined aircraft suitable for inter-island work. Design of the prototype Islander began in 1963, the first metal cut in 1964, and the high wing piston-engined plane for pilot and nine passengers completed its seventy minute maiden flight on 13 June 1965. In 1979 the company was bought by Pilatus Aircraft of Switzerland and now trades under the name of Pilatus Britten-Norman. Bruce Jacob started in the tool-making department, worked in the design office, in production control, and is now the airfield's operations manager. He is also company health and safety adviser and in charge of airport security.

rejection. When you have an aircraft proven, and development still going on after thirty years, you'd think we had proved ourselves and money would be forthcoming.

I would very much like to see an air service for the Isle of Wight. I've sat on the Island Air Panel here for five or six years, but we never seem to reach a conclusion other than it's going to cost a lot of money. The panel meets very infrequently and each time there's a different set of councillors who all ask the same questions. I can't understand why the idea isn't taken up. Having the business would need an infrastructure of cars and roads and create a lot of employment. Many people have their own aircraft or hire them – forty to fifty planes coming here on some Sundays is not unusual – and we sometimes ask them why they come. 'Oh,' they say, 'just to have a walk in the fresh air; everything's slower over here and we enjoy it.' Then they ask us for a taxi and go off somewhere for lunch. It would be nice if more people could come and see us for the day like that.

Tony Roden, 55, was born in Birmingham, trained to be a mechanical engineer and worked in Crawley New Town, Sussex, and central London before coming to work in the Isle of Wight. He is now Public Relations Manager for Westland Aerospace Ltd in East Cowes. He is married to his second wife and they have three children.

Westland's Public Relations Manager

[Westland Aerospace is a world leader in the design and manufacture of engine nacelles (streamlined enclosures on an aircraft to accommodate engines) for regional turbo-prop aircraft. It is owned by the multi-national giant GKN, and is a member of a UK Industrial Support Group of thirty-six aerospace companies, which has joined forces with Lockheed Martin to produce the next generation C–13OJ Hercules.]

This company started as Sam Saunder's Boatyard in the late 1890s, building wooden boats and pioneering the technique of strong light-weight hulls. In 1911 Saunders built a boat and plane combined and called it the Bat Boat, the first record of an amphibious vehicle made on this site. The company became Saunders-Roe, and went on to develop flying boats and pioneer helicopters. Then along came Westland Aircraft, which took over the company in the early 1960s. The government was trying to rationalize the aircraft industry by putting helicopter companies under

Westland, and fixed-wing aircraft with the then British Aircraft Corporation (now British Aerospace). Sir Christopher Cockerell invented the hovercraft, and we developed it for him and received the first contract in the 1950s from the Ministry of Technology.

There are about 1,200 people working here now. I think we're the biggest industrial employer on the Island. Our site has a very important waterfront but we don't build anything now that needs access to water and we'd like to sell it and move elsewhere on the Island. We've increased the value of the site by getting planning permission for a hotel, conference centre, shops and a marina, a scheme that is important for the Isle of Wight as a whole, as well as for our company because we need to raise money to pay for the development of new programmes. A new development on the waterfront would make East Cowes a much better place. It's better than it was ten years ago. It was a dump then, a disgrace. The company was responsible for the poor maintenance of buildings and we have made a big effort to modernize their appearance.

Our turnover is £200 million a year and we plough in excess of about £30 million a year into the Isle of Wight economy. But I haven't seen any government support for this company for a long time. To be in the aircraft business today you have to have access to large sums of money. A programme we're planning would mean having to put up £30 million. We have five new programmes, all in similar phases, so their earnings are huge in potential. But it's a long-term business and you need a lot of capital. The government has a policy of non-intervention and the aerospace industry understand that, but you must have a policy.

[In November 1995 GKN announced that the management of five new operating businesses would be centred on the Isle of Wight and Westland Aerospace would be known as GKN Westland Aerospace.]

The Radar Man

Plessey have occupied the 52 acre site at Cowes since the early '60s and have developed the business to such an extent that, when GEC made a take-over bid for the

Roger Barnes, 50, studied mechanical engineering and got a First Class Honours degree at Imperial College. He joined Plessey in 1967 during his university holidays, and returned for seven years after he left college. He subsequently worked for companies that included Vickers, Tube Investments and GEC. In 1983 he rejoined Plessey on the Isle of Wight and is now managing director of the air defence division of Siemens Plessey Systems. He is married to Angela, a former marketing director of the Isle of Wight Development Board, and they have one daughter.

company in the mid-1980s, many people saw the economy of the Island seriously threatened. We have employed about 1,200 people on this site for the last fifteen years. In fact, that bid was defeated and eventually Siemens, a Germany company, took over the ownership of Plessey's Radar business. In 1989 we became Siemens Plessey Systems but we still retain our British identity.

In Germany they approach problems differently. Their policies are long-term. Under Plessey, we were for ever being asked to maximize our results every quarter, because of the impact they might have on share prices on the stock exchange. Now, with Siemens, we have a more stable environment, but of course a very different culture. For the first two or three years we failed to come to terms with this – the British characteristic of entrepreneurial spirit being at considerable variance with the more methodical German approach.

At Cowes we design and develop radar for civil and military use and have produced over 2,000 installations in over 100 different countries. We are the leading UK surveillance radar company, and are the prime supplier to all three branches of Her Majesty's forces and NATO northern region. The key project for us here at present is called MESAR – Multi-function Electronically Scanned Adaptive Radar – a programme we've worked on for fourteen years. This provides radars for the twenty-first century when the threat from a missile or aircraft is going to be much more sophisticated and difficult to detect.

Radars in the past have either performed a surveillance or a tracking role. Our leap forward is to have taken all the existing separate functions and combined them into one which still works in the face of extensive enemy jamming. There is no radar in the world that can do this to the extent we can.

The annual total turnover of Siemens Plessey Systems is around £300 million and of that the Isle of Wight contributes about half. The nature of our equipment is very sensitive, and individual orders are usually in excess of £5 million, with others reaching ten times that amount.

It's not a disadvantage to have a company like this on the Isle of Wight because the cost of ferrying our product across the water is of less significance than it would be with, say, washing machines or television sets. This is an excellent site to show customers what we do and we don't have recruitment or maintenance problems. We employ 350 to 400 graduate engineers, the vast majority from the mainland. Some come for interviews and say: love the job, but couldn't live on an island. Not that many, though. If you're a sailor, it's a heaven-sent location. If you love the countryside and walking and peace and quiet, it's terrific. The negative side is that there isn't the choice of entertainment.

We are dealing with technology that does amazing things, and the applications of this technology are very sobering when you recognize they can make the difference between war and peace, a country retaining its independence or losing a lifetime of tradition.

Mr Randini – The Magic Man

I had a twelve year apprenticeship with my father doing illusions, children's work, sawing people in half, floating, but I probably did my first solo magic performance when I was about ten at a magicians' dinner in Ryde. My brother was interested in Punch and Judy and I used to get dragged along to watch. I never liked it as a child. I didn't like the noise and my Punch and Judy is less violent than the ones I saw. It is slapstick – in fact the stick that's used is called a slapstick and that's where the term came from. Most of my work on the Island now is as a children's entertainer.

David Rann, 32, was born on the Isle of Wight. His father, known as the Great Randini, has been performing magic on the Island for forty-five years, and David, the youngest of three children, was the fifth member of the family to join him on stage. He (David) worked in a butcher's shop for six years, became a professional magician in 1986 and is now a full-time magician and Punch and Judy man. He has worked in China, America, Monte Carlo, Spain, France, the Canaries and Madeira. He is married to Laura and they have a young son.

I learnt Mr Punch's voice, the most important part of a traditional Punch and Judy, from my brother. It's a secret technique – you have to put something into the back of the throat – and although a lot of people now know what is used to make the noise, it doesn't mean they can actually do it. They say you're not a true Punch and Judy man until you've swallowed three of these 'gadgets'.

When I was younger I met a lot of Punch and Judy men who told me everyone used to throw their pennies in the hat at the end, and now in the '90s, they still only throw in pennies. So it's very difficult to make a living. Many do it by introducing a balloon or a cuddly toy, to sell at the end. But I feel they're turning a performance into a pitchman's gimmick and I don't do that. People know that if they sit and watch me, no one's going to come round with a hat. They won't have to pay anything because I'm a professional entertainer and get paid by the people who book me.

Punch and Judy dates back about 325 years. It started with real people, not puppets, in Italy, and was called Punchinello. Much of what we say is traditional, wasn't actually in the original. The policeman wasn't around 325 years ago. I'm not sure about the sausages, but I think there was a crocodile. The original ones had the hanging and coffin scene, which I don't. I think you have to try and change with the times, but keep the tradition as much as possible. Children shout more in anticipation of Punch going to knock someone over the head than when he actually does it, and I do as little knocking as possible. When I come out of the show, nine times out of ten the first thing children will say to me is, 'Did the crocodile eat the sausages?', which to them is the naughtiest thing they see.

I think entertaining children today is a responsibility and privilege. If I tell a child to go and throw a ball into the street, he will because Mr Randini, the magician, said so. So if Mr Randini says, 'Don't take sweets from strangers', my voice is very important. Sometimes I think they expect me to do magic when I meet them in the supermarket. To adults I'm just the entertainer. But to children, I'm Mr Randini, the magic man.

Index